God Is All Joy
Life of St. Teresa of the Andes

God Is All Joy
Life of St. Teresa of the Andes

Jennifer Moorcroft

ICS Publications
Washington, D. C.
2009

© Washington Province of Discalced Carmelites Inc., 2009

ICS Publications
2131 Lincoln Road, NE
Washington, DC 20002-1199
www.icspublications.org

Typeset and produced in the United States of America

Library of Congress Cataloging-in-Publication Data

Moorcroft, Jennifer.
God is all joy : life of Saint Teresa of the Andes / by Jennifer
Moorcroft.
    p. cm.
Includes bibliographical references.
ISBN 0-935216-42-1 (alk. paper)
    1. Teresa, de los Andes, Saint, 1900-1920.   2. Christian
saints--Chile
--Biography.   I. Title.
BX4700.T395M66 2006
282.092--dc22
[B]
                        2006017084

Contents

Introduction.. vii

Chapter 1: Born in the Midst of Riches 1

Chapter 2: A Cloudless Day... 9

Chapter 3: I Asked Him to Take Me 17

Chapter 4: The Happiest Age to Be 23

Chapter 5: I Want to Be a Carmelite............................. 31

Chapter 6: Child of Mary.. 39

Chapter 7: Dear Old Algarrobo..................................... 55

Chapter 8: Last Days at School..................................... 61

Chapter 9: Life at Home 69

Chapter 10: Los Andes Carmel..................................... 81

Chapter 11: Preparing for Carmel................................. 89

Chapter 12: Last Days at Home.................................... 101

Chapter 13: First Days in Carmel 109

Chapter 14: Cenacle Retreat 119

Chapter 15: Clothing Day 129

Chapter 16: Novitiate... 139

Chapter 17: Last Days.. 149

Chapter 18: First Fruits 155

Bibliography 163

Introduction

A few years ago I was sent a prayer card of Chile's first canonized saint, Teresa of Jesus of the Andes. On the back was a short biography. It told of a vibrant young woman who loved sports and music, and with a wide circle of friends, who entered Carmel and who died only eleven months later at the age of nineteen.

Some time later, I saw in a newspaper the photo of a young Chilean girl praying at her shrine. The caption said that each month more than 100,000 visitors flock to the shrine, many of them young people. I was intrigued. What was it about this young woman, barely out of school, that drew so many people to her and that was so outstanding that she was now a canonized saint?

The answer began to appear some time later when I read a series of books by Fr. Michael Griffith—her letters and diary, testimonies, short biographical sketches, sermons and homilies. She shone through these pages as a delightful and exceptional young person, one whose radiant life should be much more widely known outside of her native Chile. Her own people love her because she is "one of them." The young people love her because she became a saint by living the same sort of life as they do, attending school, playing sports, enjoying her friends, and through it all, living her faith to the fullest.

She is a saint for the Americas, for the new world. When the Church canonizes someone, this is not simply because of that person's outstanding holiness, but because She believes that that particular person has a special message, a relevance, for us today. A saint for the Americas is very timely. The highest percentage of Catholics are there, but the Catholic Faith is increasingly at risk, with thousands of

Evangelical Christians pouring down from the United States to evangelize those whom they see as hardly Christian at all. The Catholics of South America are often viewed as being but imperfectly converted from paganism, conquered and converted unwillingly by the sword of the conquistadores. Their Catholic Faith is frequently portrayed as being a veneer, beneath which they cling far more deeply to their old beliefs.

Sometimes there may be an element of truth in all this, but the life of Saint Teresa of the Andes shows that this is far from being the whole truth. Juanita, as she was known, came from a deeply religious family, whose Catholic faith was genuinely and sincerely held, and which survived and triumphed despite the many problems the different members of her family had. In the wide circle of her friends, many followed her into the religious life or devoted themselves to a generous Christian apostolate of social concern and activity in the world.

All this was not based on a shallow, half-pagan belief, but rather, as Juanita's schooling demonstrated, on a thorough grounding, not only in theology, but also in philosophy, logic and the humanities. Even more importantly, it was at the same time informed by a fervent and disciplined spiritual life centered on the sacraments and above all on the presence of Jesus in the Blessed Sacrament. Theologians, reading the writings of this nineteen year old girl, are amazed at the profound, reasoned and clear understanding she had of her faith, a faith that was vibrantly set on fire by her total love for God.

We in the West need her, too. Over the decades there seems to have been a determined conspiracy to undermine and weaken the Catholic Faith. The media frequently portrays Catholics as narrow-minded, joyless, bigoted, repressed and marginalized--the list could go on. Teresa's life, on the contrary, bears witness that a life totally lived for the love of Christ is radiant, joyous and life-expanding.

There is in addition the constant and determined undermining of the role and importance of the family, even though statistics show unequivocally that it is the best way to bring up children and is the main stabilizing force in society. It is only very grudgingly that even the word *marriage* is allowed to appear in official documents dealing with family life.

Teresa's family was far from being exempt from the suffering and dilemmas that beset our world; they had severe financial problems, for example. Her brother Luis lost his faith for a long time through philosophical doubts, her father stopped practicing his faith, her brother Miguel was the wayward black sheep of the family; they had to cope with sickness and death. That they all returned to the Faith shows that the strength of faith has power to triumph over the many ills that beset our modern world as it triumphed over the problems they faced. The prayers of their daughter brought them through all their trials, because they saw in her the reality of the love of God that would not let them go.

In our schools, our children are being taught more about other religions than they are about the Christian faith. Christianity, especially, has to be shown as just one option among many, and as a form of belief that is irrelevant, marginalized and based on outmoded superstition and myth. It definitely can't appeal to a rational human being or be seen as a genuine way of life. In general, understanding of the Christian faith has been so watered down that the remnants of it vaguely known by most of the population are but a caricature of the real thing, and Catholic Christianity even more so. People seeking some form of spirituality therefore tend to seek it elsewhere, especially in the variety of New Age beliefs and practices. Even in Catholic schools the Faith can be watered down to an insipid broth that nourishes no one.

And yet, the Catholic Faith has a richness, a depth, a variety and a wholeness that is unrivalled and profoundly satisfying. Teresa herself received that sound training in her faith that was the foundation of her exceptional life of prayer, self-giving and union with God. Despite her youth, her ability to grasp and explain her faith proved an irresistible magnet to her friends and to those she taught in her catechism classes. But above all, she was in love with God, crazy in love with him, and this was most catching of all.

That is why I wanted to tell her story, so that others, too, may catch the love of God from her and find the joy and happiness that living in the love of God gives, even when that means following him to calvary as she did.

I wish to thank Father Michael Griffin for his encouragement and support in writing this account. It was solely to his books on Saint Teresa of the Andes and for all the material they provided, that I was able to turn. Without them this book could not have been written.

Chapter 1
Born in the Midst of Riches

On 3 April 1987, Pope John Paul II came to Chile and, in the beautiful O'Higgins Park in the heart of Santiago, beatified a young woman who would, six years later, become Chile's first canonized saint. This was during the Pinochet era, and the brutality of that regime marred the celebrations. During the Mass, as the Gospel was being read, which was the Beatitudes, young protestors and demonstrators moved in to draw attention to their political demands. Police quickly moved in, discharging tear gas to quell the demonstrators, and the Pope continued the Mass, his eyes still streaming from the effects of the tear gas.

It was a poignant moment. On the one hand, young people who, rightly, wanted radical change in their country but felt that only militancy could further their cause. On the other hand, the celebration of a young woman, to be known as Teresa of Jesus of the Andes, who equally wanted radical change, but who knew that the transformation she sought could start only in a heart that is open to the love of God.

As the Pope said in his homily, "Blessed Teresa gives us a message of reconciliation: 'There are three things that last—faith, hope and charity—and the greatest of these is love.' These words of Saint Paul, the culmination of his hymn to charity, resound with new tones in this Eucharistic celebration. Yes, the greatest of these is love."[1]

In a few deft words, the Pope painted a concise and beautiful portrait of Teresa of the Andes, as she is popularly known. "For her, God is infinite joy. This is the new hymn of Christian love that arises spontaneously from the soul of this young Chilean girl, in whose glorified face we can sense the grace of her transformation in Christ. In her

1

we see the virtue of understanding, serving, humble and patient love, which never destroys human values, but rather elevates and transfigures them."[2]

Teresa of the Andes was born in Santiago on 13 July 1900. Juanita, as she was always known in the family, was the fourth child of seven children, although one sister, Juana, died a few hours after birth.

Both her parents, Miguel Fernandez Jarequamada and Lucia Solar Armstrong, came from large families themselves. Her father was the eighth of fifteen children, and her mother was the second of ten children and, as her surname suggests, had British ancestry. It was a difficult birth, and her mother feared the baby would not survive. But Juanita was a fighter, and Ladisloa, the family coachman, remarked that "if this little girl came this far, it is a sign that the Lord wants her to do great things."

The eldest of the children was Lucia, and then came two boys, Miguel and Luis. After Juanita there were Rebecca and Ignacio. Of all her brothers and sisters, Juanita was closest to her younger sister Rebecca and her older brother Luis. Within the family circle they formed a permanent and indestructible trio, as Luis termed it, although they differed widely in character. Rebecca's character was sunny and expansive and she loved parties, while Luis was much more thoughtful and philosophical. Juanita described herself as timid, gentle and sensitive, but she was also a born leader, energetic and enthusiastic for life.

The family was wealthy and aristocratic. "Jesus did not desire me to be poor like himself," Juanita said. "I was born in the midst of riches, spoiled by all."[3] It was also both a close-knit family and a large one, with numerous aunts and uncles and cousins.

Two days after her birth, on the eve of the Feast of Our Lady of Mount Carmel, 15 July, Juanita was baptized in the parish church.

There was a family dispute over her name, but it was eventually agreed to call her Juana Enriqueta Josephina de los Sagrados Corazones. Her long name tells us much about her deeply devout family. Juana was the name of her maternal grandmother, who had died three years previously, Enriqueta the name of her paternal grandmother. She was given the name of Josephina because of her mother's devotion to St. Joseph, and the dedication of "de los Sagrados Corazones"—of the Sacred Hearts—because of both her parents' devotion to the Sacred Hearts of Jesus and Mary.

For the first seven years the family lived with their maternal grandfather, Don Eulogio Solar, who was a doctor, in his mansion on Rosas Street, Santiago, where Juanita was born. It was an extended household, for besides Juanita's family, there were also living there her mother's younger brother, Francis; her aunt, Juanita Solar, with her six children; and another aunt, Teresa Vicuña, who had two children. With so many young children, there was plenty of noise and laughter, as well as squabbles and fights. Juanita would always be in the thick of things. She loved to join in games that her brothers organized, and sometimes her mother had to rescue her from them to prevent her getting hurt. Not that Juanita would have minded. She played to win and usually did.

The first change in her life came when she was six, and went briefly to school for the first time. Her grandfather didn't want Juanita and her younger sister Rebecca to start school at such an early age, but their mother insisted. Juanita was sent to the school run by the Carmelite Sisters of Saint Teresa on Saint Dominic Street, in the afternoons. However, the experiment was not a happy one and lasted only one month. One of the little girls at the school bullied the other children, and Juanita, among others, was the butt of her spitefulness. Well able to come to the rescue of one of her little cousins who was also at the school, she would not defend herself. One of the bully's favorite tricks was to try to pull Juanita's veil off in chapel, which would have been especially trying for Juanita, who was already feeling drawn to prayer and the presence of Jesus in the Eucharist. She had always been encouraged to tell her mother everything, so in all innocence told her mother about the bullying. When her mother complained to the Superior, this was interpreted as telling tales, for which, to her bewilderment, Juanita was punished. However, when her mother found out about the punishment, she withdrew her daughter from the school. Juanita had a few more months to be at home with the family and the routine she loved.

A deep religious faith was the bedrock of the home in Rosas Street. Juanita described her grandfather as always having a rosary in his hand, and from an early age she loved to hear stories of God, of talk about the faith, of priests and nuns.

Above all, from the age of six, shortly before the earthquake in 1906, she started going with her mother and her aunt Juana to daily Mass. They explained the different ceremonies to her, and the significance of the Mass. From then on, her one longing was to receive Holy Communion. Juanita remembered sitting at the table back home with her mother and aunt while they asked her questions to see whether she really understood. She did indeed, but canon law at that time did not allow children to receive communion at such an early age. However much she pleaded, the reply was always, "You are too young." She had another four long years to wait.

The year 1907 saw profound changes in her life. Their grandfather had a magnificent hacienda in Chacabuco, to the north of Santiago, set in 23,000 acres of land, where the family spent their vacations in the early summer. It was a paradise for the children. They could go for walks in the mountains, they learned to ride, and they had acres of land to explore. The family went there that year as usual, together with Aunt Teresa and her two children, and her grandfather. Every evening, Juanita recalled, her grandfather made them mount a horse, flipping a coin to see who would be first. Rebecca always won. However, the holidays were abruptly interrupted when Don Eulogio was suddenly stricken with paralysis. Aunt Teresa went back with him to Santiago, leaving the youngest children at the hacienda in the care of "Mama" Ofelia Miranda, Juanita's dearly loved "Mamita," the trusted servant who looked after her.

Don Eulogio died on 13 May while Mass was being said for him in an oratory at the side of his room. He was in some spiritual distress as Mass began; then, at the Consecration, he died peacefully. "His death was that of a saint," remarked Juanita later in her diary, "as was his life."[4]

The news arrived at Chacabuco in the middle of the night; Juanita was woken up and told of her grandfather's death, although they left Luis to sleep on, as he was very ill at the time. Instead, Juanita went to him in the morning with the news, saying, "He's gone now." When the servants came to dress Luis they did not tell him about his grandfather, trying to keep everything as normal as possible. Luis, however, was so upset that he began to cry and shout, "Why didn't they tell me? My grandfather is dead."

The children were taken back to Santiago, where they saw their beloved grandfather's empty room, and the reality of their loss sank in. He had indeed gone from them.

After the burial his estates were divided up between the various families. The house and the farm were auctioned off, dividing it in perpetuity into three smaller estates. Juanita's mother inherited the estate at Baños. The family had several homes in Santiago—one at the corner of Cathedral and Teatinos, a stately home on Ejercito Avenue that had belonged to their maternal grandmother, and a third one on Vergara Street near the Alameda. After Don Eulogio's death the family moved to 1646 Santo Domingo Street, and lived there for about five years. To their great distress, the hacienda at Chacabuco, where the family had spent so many wonderful holidays, had to be auctioned off due to a business mistake made by their father. When they went there for the last time, Juanita became very ill and her aunt gave Juanita a porcelain statue of Our Lady of Lourdes to keep by her bedside, provided she would drink her medicine. Juanita treasured this statue, and gave it, when she entered Carmel, to her favorite brother Luis. "She has been my intimate confidante from the tenderest years of my life," Juanita wrote in a long letter accompanying the statue. "She used to listen to me when I told her of my joys and sorrows. So many times she comforted my heart when it was weighed down with sorrow."[5] Luis kept it until his own death as a precious reminder of his sister. Juanita dated her devotion to Our Lady from this time. Every day Luis invited her to say the rosary with him, and they both made a promise to recite it for the rest of their lives. Juanita recalled only one time, when she was little, when she forgot to say it, an omission that really upset her.

Once they were settled in Santo Domingo Street Juanita became a day student at the school run by the Sacred Heart sisters on the Alameda, a beautiful colonial street lined with elm trees. It was known as the French School because the sisters had come from France and there was an emphasis on the French language. Her parents had already recognized that Juanita was highly intelligent and gifted, and wanted her to benefit from the school's excellent academic record. The school's focus was on providing a balanced and sound grounding in both the classic humanities, which included philosophy, logic, ontology and psychology, and religious education. This depth and balance are reflected in Juanita's writings, which are remarkable in such a young person, and reflect the high quality of the religious education she received.

She was a remarkable all-rounder. Although physical education and sports were not a priority at the school, Juanita was extremely fond of a variety of sports and excelled at them. Her main passion was horseback riding, and she was an excellent tennis player and swimmer.

She was also a fine musician, with a melodious alto voice. She learned to play the guitar and also the organ. There was one in the private chapel at the Chacabuco hacienda, and when the estate was sold the organ was given to her and installed in her room. Her brother Luis, whose room was next to hers, recalled the pleasure it gave him to hear her playing on it very softly each morning when she woke up. When he asked her why she played it at that time of the day, she responded that "It is such a joy when I wake up to greet God by singing."

Later that year the sisters at her school prepared her for her first confession and, two years later, in 1909, she and Luis were confirmed by Bishop Baldomero Grossi in the Cathedral at Santiago. Now, there was the greatest wish of her heart to look forward to, the day of her First Holy Communion.

Notes

1. Quoted in Michael D. Griffin, O.C.D., *God the Joy of My Life: A Biography of Saint Teresa of Jesus of the Andes with the Saint's Spiritual Diary*, 3rd ed. (Teresian Charism Press: Hubertus, WI, 1995), "Papal Homily at the Beatification of Sister Teresa of the Andes," p. 319.

2. *God the Joy of My Life*, p. 321.

3. *Diary* 2 (found above in *God the Joy of My Life*). Hereafter "*Diary*."

4. *Diary* 4

5. *Diary* 81

Chapter 2
A Cloudless Day

For four long years, as she went to daily Mass with her mother and aunt, Juanita had yearned for the privilege of Holy Communion. First confession and Confirmation were stepping-stones on the way to that goal, but above all there was a daily determination to make herself as ready as she could for that longed-for day. There were patterns of behavior that she knew hurt her Lord, childish though they were.

First among these were her occasional outbursts of temper. The other children, knowing that she was normally very even tempered, would try and provoke her by deliberately doing and saying things that would make her angry. She rarely rose to their bait, pretending she couldn't hear them. Although this pleased her mother, the effort of trying to control her fiery temper was obviously a great strain. If something happened afterwards that she didn't like, she would burst into tears and hysterical sobbing.

There were fights with her brothers, and her mother would sometimes have to intervene to bring them together and make them put things right. Only with Luis did she never fight. She had strong reactions to people and events she didn't like. In her own words, they made her blood boil. There was one of her mother's cousins, Rosenda Luco Solar, for example, whom she said she couldn't stand. When she stayed with them at Chacabuco, Rosenda spoiled Rebecca, which made Juanita jealous and upset.

"I was terrible with her," Juanita recalled, "and I did not bear with her in any way."[1] However, her mother said that actually Juanita was always very sweet with her, which shows the effort she made not to let her feelings be known.

She also found it difficult to do what she was told, dragging her feet when asked to do things she didn't like, and then taking her time carrying out her little tasks. Her brother Luis described their mother as "a demanding authoritarian," so it could have been a case of the clash of two strong wills!

With light brown hair and blue eyes—inherited, perhaps from her British ancestry—Juanita was very attractive, and she was often being told that she was the prettiest of the children. Her mother was afraid that all the adulation would make her vain, and Juanita herself wasn't immune to the flattery. "God alone knows what it cost me to overcome this pride or vanity that took possession of my heart," Juanita admitted.[2]

When, in 1909, she was told that she could make her First Holy Communion in a year's time, provided she prepared herself for it, Juanita made a determined effort to change. Now she carried out her tasks without being told. Despite provocation, she wouldn't get involved with the children's fights and squabbles, even if she had to bite her lips hard to control herself. As was the custom of the time, she wrote all her "acts of virtue" down in a notebook—and filled it full.

By June, the month of the Sacred Heart, she had changed so much that her mother agreed she should make her First Communion. The date was set for 11 September 1910. First, though, Juanita made a retreat at her school, and then, when she returned home, a week before the great day, she continued the retreat at home, asking to have her meals by herself in her room. As her mother recalled, "She outdid herself in everything. Her retreat was one of great recollection, and when she got home from school she would go and stay in her room. It brought tears to our eyes. She seemed more like a little angel."[3]

The evening before, Juanita made a general confession, and then went to each member of the household, from her father to the humblest servant, and begged their pardon for all her faults. She also wrote a touching letter to her parents:

> Thanks for all the kindnesses I've received from you, and for bringing me to this school. Here they are teaching me to be good and pious, and above all they prepared me to make my First Communion.
>
> Right now the only thing left for me to do is to beg your pardon for all the acts of disobedience I've committed and for all my complaining. I hope I'll never do it again.
>
> Your little daughter who loves you so much
> Juana Fernandez Solar[4]

The great day dawned, cloudless and sunny; Juanita got up early, too excited to stay in bed. Usually her mamita, Ofelia Miranda, would help her to dress, but today her mother came to help her put on her long, white communion dress.

When the communicants arrived at their school, where the ceremony was to take place, they prayed the rosary, but instead of the Hail Mary they recited, "Come, my Jesus, come. Oh, my Savior, come Yourself to prepare my heart." Then they processed two by two into the chapel. Juanita's mother headed the procession, with Monsignor Jara, the chaplain, bringing up the rear. Their kneelers were covered in fine white cloth, with a candle and a white lily at the side.

Monsignor Jara's sermon made such an impression on Juanita that she could recall it some years later. "You are approaching to become witnesses of the intimate union of your souls with Jesus Christ," he told them. "Look at the angels of the altar, dear little girls. Look at them, they envy you. All heaven is present."[5]

"It is impossible to describe what took place between my soul and Jesus," Juanita wrote afterwards about receiving her first Holy Communion. "I asked him a thousand times that he would take me, and I experienced his dear voice for the first time. 'Oh Jesus I love you, I adore you!' I prayed to him for everybody. And I felt the Virgin near me. Oh, how my heart expanded! For the first time I experienced a delicious peace."[6]

After they had made their thanksgiving, all the children went out on to the patio to be with their families and give out gifts to the poor. Then on their return home there was a steady stream of friends and exchanging of presents, until Juanita's bed and bureau were laden with gifts.

The day marked her definitively. "Daily contact with Our Lord in Holy Communion transformed her," said Luis. Even her brothers and sisters noticed the change in her. She had always been a leader, with a character that attracted others to her, but now her qualities of gentleness, helpfulness and obedience began to rub off on them, too.

She said, "I experienced his dear voice for the first time." In a letter to the Jesuit Father Antonio Maria Falgueras written a few years later, Juanita described in detail what she experienced. She implies in this letter that before her First Holy Communion she regularly heard Our Lady's voice:

> Since I was about seven years old, there was a very great devotion born in my soul to my Mother, the Most Holy Virgin. I told her everything that happened to me, and she spoke to me. I heard her voice clearly and distinctly in my soul. She advised me and told me what I must do to please Our Lord. I thought that this was something natural, and it never occurred to me to speak of what the Most Holy Virgin was telling me. From the time of my First Communion, Our Lord spoke to me after Communion and told me things I'd never suspected; and even when I asked him, he would tell me things that were going to happen, and then they

really did occur. But I went on thinking that everybody
who went to Communion was treated this way.[7]

Only when she happened to mention to her mother something Our
Lord had said to her did Juanita realize that her experience was exceptional. It alarmed her mother, who urged her to speak to her director,
Father Colom, also a Jesuit priest, but at that point Juanita was too
distressed herself, and too shy, to do so. Much later, she wrote a letter
to one of her friends that described the sort of locutions she received,
although they became less frequent towards the end of her life:

> There is another kind of prayer, and it is called a lo-
> cution. This consists in interiorly experiencing a voice
> that seems to be, now Our Lord or the Most Holy Vir-
> gin, telling us what we should do to be good, or to do
> something else. Sometimes it is our own understand-
> ing itself rapidly reading things; at other times, it is
> Our Lord inspiring us. Nevertheless, the only thing we
> should pay attention to is the good received from that
> communication, without trying to figure out whether
> it comes from God or from our own reason. Also, we
> should do only what is in harmony with God's will;
> since the devil often inspires in us things that, though
> they may not be evil in themselves, may harm our
> souls. As an example: excessive penances. When one
> experiences that kind of prayer, you should check with
> your confessor about what you hear interiorly.[8]

Juanita was speaking from her own experience. She was always
meticulous in seeking the advice of her confessors, consulting them on
her prayer and penances, keeping them fully informed of her progress
in the spiritual life. Her one fear was that she was being deceived. She
knew also from her own experience how the devil could try to trick her

by false voices. In the letter to Fr. Antonio she describes one such occasion, which demonstrates her spiritual maturity and discernment:

> I recognized very clearly my Most Holy Mother's voice and my good Jesus' voice. Once I was in doubt; I asked something of the Most Holy Virgin; and I heard another, a very different voice from the one I had been accustomed to hearing, a voice that I still remember. This voice did not counsel me to do good and left me very disturbed. Then with all my soul I invoked the Most Holy Virgin and she answered me, saying that the devil had answered me and that, in the future, I should always ask whether it was she who was speaking to me. But this never happened again.[9]

Shortly after Juanita made her First Holy Communion, the family moved from their home in Santo Domingo Street to one of their other homes, 475 Ejercito Street. This move was caused by some further reverses the family had suffered in their financial situation. Her grandfather, Don Eulogio, as well as being a doctor, had been a financial genius in buying up real estate and in administering the properties he had acquired. Juanita's father, however, was no businessman. He made some unfortunate mistakes in handling the financial affairs of the estates he had inherited on the death of Don Eulogio, halving the family fortune. They were not by any means destitute, but it did mean they had to sell of some of their property, reduce the number of servants and rein in considerably their former lavish lifestyle.

Notes

1. *Diary* 5
2. *Diary* 2
3. Michael D. Griffin, O.C.D. comp., *Testimonies to Saint Teresa of the Andes*, 2nd ed. (Teresian Charism Press, Hubertus, WI, 1995), p. 59. Hereafter *"Testimonies"* with page reference.
4. Letter 1 in *Letters of Saint Teresa of Jesus of the Andes*, trans. Michael D. Griffin, O.C.D. (Teresian Charism Press: Hubertus, WI, 1994). Hereafter cited as *"Letter"* with respective number.
5. *Diary* 6
6. *Diary* 6
7. *Letter* 87
8. *Letter* 138
9. *Letter* 87

Chapter 3
I Asked Him to Take Me

"I asked him a thousand times that he should take me," Juanita wrote of her First Communion. "From that day on the earth no longer held any attraction for me. I wanted to die and begged Jesus that he'd take me on 8 December."[1] Indeed, she was convinced that this was the date on which she would die, and for three years, from 1912 to 1914, she was seriously ill on 8 December, Feast of the Immaculate Conception.

In 1912, when she was twelve, she became critically ill with diphtheria, and there was a genuine fear for her life. A few years earlier, a young aunt of hers, Maria, had already died of the illness when she, too, was only twelve years old. Maria had led a remarkably penitential life in her few short years, and as she lay dying she was in ecstasy, her face radiant, saying repeatedly, "How great, how immense God is." The smile on her lips remained after death. It was no surprise that this account of her death affected Juanita very deeply.

The following year Juanita had a high fever, and the year after that she went down with appendicitis, which at that time was a life-threatening condition. She had to stay off school, "and for this I was very happy!" she wrote.[2]

By 24 December she was in increasing pain, and it was decided she should have an operation. She was transferred to St. Vincent's on the 28th. Juanita found this very distressing, because in the event of death she did not want to die away from her own home; moreover, she didn't at all like the idea of being in a bed slept in by other people.

The operation was set for 30 December, and early that morning she received Holy Communion, asking the Lord for the courage and

17

serenity she would need. Surrounded by her relatives, her room filled with flowers by the Sisters who ran the hospital, she was prepared for surgery. Before being taken to the operating room she kissed the statue of Our Lady, which she loved so much. Her father and Aunt Juanita were not there, as they couldn't cope with the thought that they might never see her again.

The operation was successful. However, she suffered severe after-effects from the chloroform and was convalescent for some weeks.

An incident took place while she was still at home and confined to bed, trivial in itself, but which was a decisive turning point for her. Normally the family made sure that there was always someone to keep her company, but on this particular day Lucia, her elder sister, was also sick and Elisea, the servant who was looking after Juanita, had gone to see to Lucia's needs. Juanita was envious and tearful that she wasn't getting the attention she thought she should have, and began to cry. Gazing at a picture of the Sacred Heart she then heard Our Lord say to her, "What! I, Juanita, am alone on the altar for love of you, and you can't even suffer one moment of solitude?"

He went on to teach her how to suffer without complaint, and then he revealed his will for her: he wanted her to become a Carmelite.

This was indeed a defining moment in her life. It deepened her already rich prayer life, and made her realize that increasing union with God meant embracing his cross joyfully and willingly. These two aspects, prayer and suffering accepted joyfully, would define her understanding of her Carmelite vocation. As she wrote later, "I don't want to weep, because I find a sacrifice bathed with tears is no sacrifice."[3] In this, she would have been much influenced by another young Carmelite, Saint Thérèse of Lisieux, whose autobiography, *The Story of a Soul*, she had begun to read and assimilate earlier that year. Thérèse was a young French Carmelite who had died in 1897 at the age of twenty-four. A year later, the autobiography she had written under obedience was beginning to be widely circulated, leading to "a storm of glory," as it has been described, and her eventual canonization as the greatest saint of modern times. She has also been made a Doctor of the Church and Patroness of the Missions. Her teaching of The Little Way has had a profound influence on modern spirituality, even beyond the Catholic Church, emphasizing as it does the path of holiness in ordinary life—doing ordinary things extraordinarily well, and total confidence in the mercy and love of God.

Juanita would appreciate Thérèse's advice to one of her novices, Marie of the Trinity, who was inclined to tears. When Thérèse pointed out the effect emotional outbursts had on community life, Marie said that from now on she would cry only before God.

Thérèse roundly disagreed. "What!" she replied, "Cry in front of God! Don't you dare behave like that; we should appear less sad with God than with people. Our kind Master has only our convents to bring joy to his heart. He comes here for rest from the constant complaints of those in the world. People in the world more often cry and complain at the Cross, and you want to be like them? It is we who should be comforting Jesus, and not he us."[4] Thérèse said that she always tried to smile when faced with something hard to bear, so that Jesus would not know how she was suffering. This message of joy in suffering was one that Juanita, too, would live to the full.

A sense of vocation had already been growing in her. Her prayer at her First Holy Communion was for the Lord to take her to himself, but she ended her account of that day with the remark that, "Jesus did not let me go but took me for himself."[5] Death was not, yet, his will for her. Before that time came he would draw her ever closer to himself in love and total self-giving, in the religious life. Nevertheless, Juanita was correct in a growing premonition that her life would indeed be short. She had to accomplish an amazing growth in holiness in a very short time.

The autobiography of Saint Thérèse of Lisieux introduced her to the Carmelite way of life, and once she had accepted his call to Carmel, her yearly episodes of severe illness ceased. When Juanita was discharged from the hospital, the family left for Chacabuco, where she could convalesce. They no longer had the hacienda, but her father had rented a house for them, and her uncle Francis also lived there.

Juanita was disappointed that because of her operation she wasn't allowed to go horseback riding; instead she drove a carriage, which she said was nearly as enjoyable. She also enjoyed the Missions that the family always arranged while they were in Chacabuco; it enabled her to go to daily Mass, which was the center of her life.

Her stay there was marred by an incident that shamed her deeply. Her older sister Lucia and a cousin decided to go swimming, but didn't want the younger children to go with them. Juanita, disgusted at being called "little" when she was, after all, fourteen years old, sulked; and when Lucia was told they had to take the younger children, Juanita decided she wouldn't go. She was ordered to go with them, but she then refused to dress until after the others had left; the girls wouldn't leave her by herself, so Juanita threw quite a tantrum. She later regretted her display of bad temper and went to apologize to her mother, who told her to go away and cry by herself. This upset Juanita even more, so that she wouldn't go in to tea until sternly ordered to do so.

The incident was really quite trivial and childish, the sort of thing that happens among children everywhere. It wasn't the sort of behavior that they had come to expect from Juanita, though, and her mother put her loss of control down to the continuing effects of the anesthetic. Juanita herself felt as if she was letting down Jesus after he had brought her through her operation. She never forgot the incident and bitterly regretted her bad behavior that day, which was now so out of character.

The family stayed in Chacabuco until March, when they returned to Santiago for the start of the school term.

Notes

1. *Diary* 6
2. *Diary* 7
3. *Letter* 88
4. Testimony of Sister Mary of the Trinity; see *Testimonies*, p. 184
5. *Diary* 6

Chapter 4
The Happiest Age To Be

"July 13. Today I'm 15 years old. Fifteen years old! The age all would like to be; the younger ones, to be considered as grownups, and the older ones...would like to return to this age because it is the happiest of all,"[1] Juanita wrote in her diary entry for that day, reflecting on the graces God had given her over the years, and that "in creating me He preferred me to millions of beings." As well as looking back, she looked forward: "The future hasn't been revealed to me, yet Jesus has pulled back the curtain and I have glimpsed the beautiful shores of Carmel." She was aware that the years ahead would bring other possibilities—marriage, becoming a teacher, perhaps. Yet Jesus had already staked his exclusive claim on her and she had no intention of following any other path. "He has kept me in solitude with Himself," she added. "Consequently, my heart, by knowing this Captain, has fallen under the spell of His love, and here He keeps me captive. Oh, how I love this prison and this powerful King who keeps me captive; and how I love this Captain who amid the waves of the ocean doesn't allow me to suffer shipwreck."[2] Daily Mass and Communion, and the interior guidance she received in prayer were the two harbor lights that would keep her unswervingly on course to the goal Jesus had willed for her.

Juanita had been encouraged to keep a diary by Madre Julia Rios, a Sacred Heart nun at Juanita's school on the Alameda. She was very fond of the sister, who provided her with wise guidance and who could already discern exceptional qualities in her young pupil. Because of a severe illness Mother Rios had been moved to the other Sacred Heart College on Maestranza Street,[3] much to Juanita's distress, for

Maestranza Street was in a different part of the city. She had written to Madre Rios about her vocation, which the nun had already suspected, and then visited her to talk things over; it was now a great disappointment that she was so far away.

However, during that term her parents told Juanita they had decided that she and Rebecca should go to the Maestranza Street College. Because of its distance from the family home, they would be going as boarders later that year.

This college was known as the English School, since the foundation had been made from the United States; the teaching of English was stressed, in contrast to her previous school of French speaking nuns.

Rebecca and Juanita began their new school in mid-July, and Juanita hated it. She found it difficult to adapt to the strict regime, and above all she missed dreadfully the close knit and lively family life she had with her parents and brothers and sisters. Nevertheless, she saw it as a preparation for that even greater separation she would have to endure when she entered Carmel, and tried to embrace it generously — even if not without complaints to her close friends!

Her holidays were overshadowed by the dread of returning to school. "I'll tell you that there are only 7 more days of vacation," she wrote to a close friend of hers, Carmen de Castro Ortuzar. "Only seven days before we must be in that dungeon. My blood runs cold just thinking about it."[4] She ended her newsy letter by urging Carmen to tear up her letter as a precaution. This was before the widespread use of the telephone, when letter writing was still a very popular pastime, and letters would often be passed around to others. Juanita did not want her distaste for school to get back to her parents or to the nuns, and she was also keeping her calling to Carmel from all but a few trusted friends and confidants.

At the boarding school, the nuns reserved the right to open both incoming and outgoing mail. In time-honored tradition the girls circumvented this inconvenience in various ways. In one of her letters to Carmen, she passed on the secret code the girls at school used. "The vowels are represented by Roman numerals," she wrote. "I is a; II is e; III is i; IV is o; V is u. Write and tell me if you like this idea or not, and whether you agree to write your letters to me in this way."[5] They also used to write their notes to each other in notebooks, which they could then pass to their friends. Even when she had left school Juanita used this system to keep in contact with friends who were still there, with Rebecca acting as a go-between. Elena Salas Gonzales, for example, was thinking of entering with the Sacred Heart nuns, while Juanita was preparing to enter the Carmelites, and they wanted to be discreet about their intentions. A fortuitous, unintended consequence of using notebooks in this way was that so many of her letters have survived, whereas they might have been thrown away if written on sheets of paper.

Despite her homesickness and the chafing discipline, Juanita did not allow her feelings to detract from her studies. The Sacred Heart College had a reputation for outstanding educational standards; she knew her parents had sent her there to benefit from the excellent education she was receiving and had no intention of letting them down. She studied hard, and easily gained top marks for those subjects she was best in. She disliked Chemistry and Physics, but nevertheless worked hard at them and managed to win the highest grades and prizes in those subjects too.

The Sacred Heart Sisters aimed to give their students a rounded education that embraced both their intellect and their spiritual life. Juanita's favorite subjects were, not surprisingly, religion, and also literature and philosophy. She was taught Latin, and spoke French

fluently. Luis testified as to the intellectual rigor of her education: "I
used to discuss the problems of Theodicy with her...She easily learned
the classic physical proof arguments for the existence of God. Even
the most difficult concepts such as potency and act, causality and
contingency were easy for her... She possessed a keen mental solidity
and a continual thirst to investigate and to know. Perhaps this aided
her in her mystical, bold and deep insights."[6]

Theology has been defined as "faith seeking knowledge," which
describes well Juanita's approach. Her faith was living and vibrant;
she wanted to love Jesus madly, love in exchange for Love: "What
love, my dear Isabel!" she wrote to one of her friends. "It is beyond
understanding. I ask myself often why all of us don't go crazy with
love for our God...On His feast day let us ask of the Divine Heart this
madness, that we may live united to Him, sing His mercies and shed
tears for His loneliness. May we at least who know Him and who have
been drawn to love Him because of His divine Word, His captivating
Beauty, His infinite Goodness, may we at least be grateful to Him."[7]

Outpourings such as these could simply be dismissed as adolescent
sentimentality, except that Juanita anchored her love for God firmly
within her whole life. True love is costly and sacrificial, and she expressed her love by trying at every moment to make herself a "good
copy of Jesus," as she put it, whatever the cost to herself.

On the other hand, theological talk of causality, contingency,
classic proofs of God, could be divorced from "real life," and easily
dismissed as irrelevant classroom dogma. True theology combines the
two. If we are in love we want to know as much as possible about the
one we love. There is external knowledge, finding out such facts as
where the person comes from, their likes and dislikes, their different
characteristics, and their views on a whole range of subjects. There is
another form of knowledge, the knowledge of the heart, which comes

from sharing our life with a person. This is not easily expressed in words and goes far deeper. In the same way, when we love God we want to know as much as possible about him, both intellectual knowledge and living, heart knowledge, and therefore come to love him even more. Head must inform heart, and heart wants to have ever deeper understanding of the one loved. As long as there are souls in love with God, such theology will never come to an end; they will never satisfy their thirst to know more of the One they love, even in heaven, for God is infinite. We shall never come to an end of discovering more of our God.

Juanita was certainly one of those souls. Thanks to the excellent theological grounding she received at school, she could express her faith and her love for God in a logical, reasoned and structured way, as all her writings demonstrate. Even more, with Saint Paul she also could say that "I know whom I have believed."[8] Her faith was truly built on rock, and expressed in all that she did and said. Her thirst for God was so strong that she loved nothing better than to discover and understand as much as she could about him. Luis said that she loved to speak of God so much that it was difficult for her to stop!

The nuns wanted their pupils to have a rounded religious education, one in which knowledge of their faith was expressed in prayer and action. Juanita and her wide circle of friends demonstrated how well they succeeded. Many entered the religious life; others married, living prayerful and dedicated family lives; others remained single and dedicated themselves to generous charitable works.

Juanita herself embarked on a very structured prayer life, strongly influenced by the Jesuits who had a house nearby, some of whom were her confessors and spiritual directors and who preached the annual retreats for the school.

Her prayer expressed itself in action. All her friends testified how generous she was in looking after the poor, as far as her means allowed, and she helped out enthusiastically with the Missions during her school holidays.

Despite being a boarder, Juanita was allowed, on occasion, to go home for a day. On one of these occasions she found that the Mother Prioress of the Carmel on Carmel Street had sent her a picture of Saint Thérèse of Lisieux, which she treasured. She had already read the *Autobiography* several times by now, strengthening her desire for the Carmelite way of life.

In September she had a decisive interview with Mother Rios. Juanita spoke frankly about her prayer and her way of life. She discussed a flirtation or *pololeo* she had had. A pololeo was a boy and girl friendship that had grown up over a period of time, but which might or might not lead to formal courtship. One boy, especially, was attracted to her, and bought her a bunch of flowers. She responded graciously, which prompted him to come round to her house, and, as was the custom, they went walking up and down in front of her house.

One reason why their mother had decided to send Juanita and Rebecca to the College on Maestranza Street was that if they had stayed at their previous school, the two girls would have had to walk past the boys' college of San Ignacio. Doña Lucia was only too aware of how attractive both her daughters were, and Rebecca was already developing a liking for party-going and flirtations. Of course, neither of the girls was cut off from male friends; their brothers had their friends, their own friends had brothers, and there were their many male cousins within their extended family. Mother Rios pointed out that having a boyfriend would be incompatible with a religious vocation, and Juanita would have to choose. Of course, there was really no contest.

Above all they discussed her vocation to Carmel. One problem that concerned them both was her health, which still continued to be poor, and which might prove an obstacle to entering such an austere order. Mother Rios's advice was to think about a religious vocation, and leave the rest to God. She also recommended that Juanita read, as well as Saint Thérèse, the works of Saint Teresa of Avila, the great Spanish saint who had reformed the Carmelite Order in the 16th century.

There were other high moments that term before the school broke up for the short autumn break. Juanita was able to attend the Profession of two Sacred Heart sisters and the Clothing ceremony of a postulant in the school chapel, which made her long for the day when she too would be a religious. A small incident she recalls in her diary[9] high-lighted her growing influence with her fellow students. A group of girls went to see Mother Rios, and Juanita, doing all she could to imagine she was in Carmel, sat on the ground rather than on a chair; the other girls followed her example, without knowing the reason for it!

Two days after her interview with Mother Rios, prizes were distributed for the end of term. Juanita came first in the handwriting contest, the first of many prizes she was to win. Because it was the end of the term, there were no lessons, so the girls played games, and went to Confession. Walking on the Alameda afterwards they bumped into Miguel, who was doing his military service, and duly admired him in his uniform.

Then they were free for ten happy days! The family set off for their beloved Chacabuco as usual. They walked all over the town seeing once more their favorite spots, they visited their Uncle Francis and some of their old servants, and met up with their cousins. They went horseback riding, flew kites, and generally enjoyed themselves. For Juanita, being able to go to Mass and receive Communion was her greatest joy.

All too soon the short break came to an end, and they returned to Santiago and the dreaded school. "Friday 24. Today we came back to school," noted Juanita in her diary. "I feel despondent and have crazy desires to cry. To you, my Jesus, I offer this pain, since I want to suffer to become like you, Jesus, my love."[10]

That term was an important milestone in her life. As part of her continuing journey towards the religious life, she asked her confessor, Fr. José Blanch, if she could make a vow of chastity. He gave her permission to make it first of all for 9 days, then to renew it periodically. She wrote out the formula of her vow:

> Today, the 8th of December 1915, at 15 years of age, I made my vow before the Most Holy Trinity and in the presence of the Virgin Mary and all the saints of Heaven, to not admit any other spouse but my Lord Jesus Christ, whom I love with all my heart and whom I desire to serve till the last moment of my life. Vow taken for the novena of the Immaculate and to be renewed with the permission of my confessor.[11]

Notes

1. *Diary* 10
2. Ibid.
3. Now Portugal Street.
4. *Letter* 5
5. *Letter* 10
6. *Testimonies*, p. 67.
7. *Letter* 109
8. 2 Tm 1:12
9. *Diary* 12
10. *Diary* 14
11. *Diary* 15

Chapter 5
I Want to Be a Carmelite

The family returned to Chacabuco in the New Year for the more extended summer holidays. Tere Jara, a cousin of theirs, was there, and Aunt Juanita joined them a little later for the Mission. Once again they enjoyed long horseback riding expeditions into the hills. One day they left at 6 o'clock in the morning, ate lunch near the mountain range, and arrived back home at eight o'clock in the evening, a round trip of some forty-five miles.

Another day they got together, meeting in one of the fields on the estate where the hay had been gathered in, and had a singing session. On other days they played games of croquet. Friends from nearby estates came over to join them, so it was a large and friendly gathering. By now they had bought a farm in Chacabuco, which they called Lourdes.

As usual, their parents arranged to have a Mission for the local workers. That year the Heart of Mary priests came to conduct it. Every day Juanita helped to run the catechism classes, which were attended by 60 children. Twenty-four of them made their First Communion, 619 people received Communion, 70 were confirmed, and there was also a wedding. The Mission ended with a procession of the Blessed Sacrament, with the farm hands forming the guard of honour.

In addition, Juanita had school assignments to complete and she tried her hand at sewing, making herself a shirt. On another day she joined forces with Rebecca to throw a banquet for friends and family. They made partridge pie, vegetable stew, little meat pies, steak with fried potatoes, and caramel cake. Juanita discovered she enjoyed domestic tasks.

As always, the thought of school cast its blight. "These happy days will turn into those sad school days that will soon be here. I get discouraged when I think of it ... I wish they'd burn the school down," she wrote to her friend Carmen. Not surprisingly she told Carmen to tear the letter up, in case it fell into the hands of Sister Popa. "I won't write any more if I hear that you haven't torn it up. What a mess it would cause."[1]

That her friends treasured her letters so much that they ignored such dire threats is something for which we can be deeply grateful, for her letters now form one of the spiritual treasures of the Church. The letter she wrote to Rebecca in April of that year, revealing her vocation as a Carmelite, is one of the most precious. So strong had her determination grown that she had to confide in someone. Juanita wrote the letter on Rebecca's fourteenth birthday, 15 April , because she felt that her sister was old enough to understand. "Believe me, Rebecca, at 14 or 15, people understand their vocation. You hear a voice and a light shows you the path of your life."[2]

Juanita told her of the vow of chastity she had made. "On the 8th of December I promised myself to Him. It's impossible to say how much I love Him. My mind is filled with Him alone. He is my ideal, my infinite ideal. I long for the day when I can go to Carmel to devote myself to Him alone."

The letter reveals the depth of her understanding of the Carmelite vocation. The decision she was describing was no youthful enthusiasm, but a mature commitment. "I see that my vocation is very great: to save souls, to give workers to Christ's vineyard." This involves sacrifice, a total self-giving. "Every sacrifice made is small compared with the value of one soul. God gave His life for them, yet how we disregard their salvation. As one betrothed to Him, I must thirst for souls, and offer my Espoused the blood He shed for each of them. And how can we win these souls? Prayer, mortification and suffering."

Above all, by love. Juanita pointed to the example of their eldest
sister Lucia, who had met Isodore, an army officer nicknamed Chiro,
whom she would eventually marry. But the depth of their love and
their union was nothing in comparison with the love of Jesus and the
union with him to which every Christian is called. "Yet, I'm just a poor
little bird without wings," she added. "And who will give me wings
so I can go and build my nest and be always close to Him? Love. Oh
yes, I love Him and I want to die for Him. My love is so great that I
would like to be martyred to prove to Him that I love Him."

Juanita had been reading the biography of another young French
Carmelite, Elizabeth of the Trinity. A younger contemporary of Thérèse
of Lisieux, she had died in 1906, after only five years as a Carmelite.
Deeply contemplative, her mission was to encourage people into a
deeper life of prayer: "I feel that my mission in heaven will be to
encourage souls to go out of themselves in order to cling to God in a
very simple and loving way," she wrote shortly before her death, "and
help them to remain in that great inner silence which allows God to
imprint himself in them and transform them into himself."[3]

This was an ideal Juanita had been living for years. "My mind is
filled with Him alone," she had written, and also that "He never leaves
me." She was spending long periods in prayer. Luis's room was next
to hers, and he said that he often opened her door and invariably found
her on her knees, motionless in prayer, and so absorbed that she was
never aware of him. Although she was normally quiet, she could also
be lively, but in church or at Mass she could easily slip into profound
stillness and prayer.

Juanita was very aware of the anguish her decision to become
a Carmelite would cause her whole family, and especially Rebecca,
with whom she was so close. But she knew that love can transcend
barriers, and if we love God, then our love for those closest to us is

strengthened because caught up into the love of God. "Your sisterly heart must break when you hear me speak of separation, when you hear me murmur that word: goodbye forever on earth that I may imprison myself in Carmel. But don't be afraid, my dear little sister. There will never be any separation between our souls. I will live in him. Search for Jesus and in him you'll find me."⁴

Later that year Juanita made a retreat based on the Ignatian Exercises. The notes of her Meditations and Colloquies are in stark contrast to the popular and richly gifted young girl that others saw. Outwardly she "had everything." "Juanita was very attractive, her way of expression was very pleasant and agreeable," Luis wrote in his Testimony. "She was quite tall, well shaped, had a certain majesty of movement, white skin, and blue eyes. … Her head was small and her hair was light brown. She had a really pleasing voice. You could recognize great strength in her deep gaze. She was a very quiet person, very much in control of herself. … Juanita was joyful and always seemed happy. Her joy was neither loud nor boisterous."⁵

She also had excellent coordination, with a grace and poise that made her an excellent athlete. Her favorite sports were horseback riding, above all, and tennis and swimming. She excelled in her studies, and in addition was very gifted musically, with a beautiful contralto voice. She was a born leader with a wide circle of friends, drawn to her by her generous, loyal, outgoing, happy and fun-loving nature.

All this could easily have made Juanita conceited and the focus of jealousy from others less gifted. However, she saw herself in the light of God, and in her diary the notes she made during this retreat reveal how far short she considered she fell in being the person she knew God wanted.

She was profoundly aware that she had been created for God's glory. This was the sole object of her life. "Why were we created? To serve and love God above all things. ... God has made His will known to me. If I fulfill it, I glorify Him, but by doing always what is most perfect."[6]

Juanita acknowledged that God had blessed her very richly, but her only concern was to use her gifts and talents for his glory, not for her own self-aggrandizement. This was in marked contrast to a certain Jansenistic tendency that sometimes prevailed in religious circles at the time. It was sometimes considered an act of humility to denigrate one's talents, and in religious orders people could be put into spheres of work to which they were not suited, and not where their natural talents would suggest. At one point Juanita's confessor asked her if she had the humility to deliberately fail her exams. Juanita's answer was "No," and only under pressure did she agree to say yes. Among the reasons she gave was that she wanted to please her parents, who were giving her such a good education and paying a lot for her costly education. She didn't want to fail her grades and give the impression that, simply because she intended becoming a Carmelite her grades didn't matter. She herself thought she was stupid, so if she did win prizes, then that was due to Jesus and Mary.

If, after doing her best, she then failed her exams, that was a different matter. This she could accept humbly, and it might have happened. She was having quite a bit of sickness that year, and Rebecca told her bluntly that she might fail her courses, that the school wasn't going to pass her, and that she would have to leave school. At first, this prospect upset her, but then she reflected that if God had at first enabled her to pass her exams and now was allowing her sickness, then, since she had been doing God's will, doing her duty, her reward would be in heaven, even if not on earth.

At the same time, Juanita was profoundly aware of what she called her "criminal nothingness." She contrasts her littleness, her misery and her many sins with the sacrifice on the cross of him who has the right to be adored and served. She was well aware that he who chose poverty, humiliation and the cross demanded the same of her, and this put all the rest in perspective.

She was also consumed with a longing for the salvation of souls, of bringing others to know and love God as she did. This was not simply a pious prayer, but something that motivated her consistently. She loved the Missions her parents ran at Chacabuco and played a full part in them. But it was her example that had the most striking effect on her friends and family, and she inspired them with her own enthusiasm and love for God. We can perhaps assess people by the friends they have, and Juanita's friends were those who loved God. Many of them followed her into the religious life; Carmen, for example, entered the Carmel of Talco. Graciela entered the Los Andes Carmel and died with a reputation for great holiness. Herminia, a second cousin and intimate friend, didn't enter the religious life, but never married. She inherited considerable wealth and gave generously to a wide range of charitable and social works. And they were by no means the only ones.

Luis said that when she was in company, although she was happy and easy to get along with, yet at the same time there was a reticence, something going on inside her, that could make her seem introverted. He himself was aware what that was, that she was taken up with the reality of God's presence within her.

Juanita ended her notes on the retreat by reaffirming her desire "that the Most Holy Trinity may come and dwell in my soul so that I can adore You and live constantly in Your presence." She made a new vow "in the presence of the Most Holy Trinity and of the Most Holy Virgin and Saint Joseph and the saints and angels of heaven; to have no other Spouse but Jesus, the only love of my soul."[7]

Notes

1. *Letter* 5
2. *Letter* 8
3. *Letter* 335 (to Sister Marie-Odile)
4 *Letter* 8
5 *Testimonies*, p. 62
6. *Diary* 17
7. *Diary* 17

Chapter 6
Child of Mary

The family went to Chacabuco at the end of the year as usual. Juanita, Luis and Rebecca took long walks on the beach discussing all manner of subjects, but Juanita and Luis also had more serious discussions together. Luis, a future lawyer, was wracked by religious doubts. He was now at the Saint Ignatius High School and strongly drawn to philosophical readings which had begun to undermine his faith.

Luis confided his doubts to Juanita, which obviously, given her own strong faith, hurt her deeply. "I am sad," she wrote in her diary for January 2nd. "My heart is bleeding. Oh, if I could, I'd offer up a thousand lives for him; my God send me all sufferings, and give me the grace to bear them so that his soul may be converted! My Jesus, I want to keep You company in the garden during Your agony. I want to console You and say with You: 'Lord, if it be possible, let this bitter chalice pass from me; but not my will but Thine be done.'"[1]

The two of them had many discussions together, but their experiences of God differed widely. Luis's avid study of philosophy increased his doubts and skepticism, whereas for Juanita philosophy grounded and deepened her faith. The wide stretches of ocean, the night skies with their myriad stars and the immense sky above the threshing fields of their estates thrilled Juanita, but for Luis they were terrifying. "Juanita would intone her favorite songs in her soft and deep voice while contemplating the stars," he recalled. "Those were unforgettable dialogues. I would ask, 'Don't you feel terror before the infinite spaces, like Pascal used to say?' Juanita answered me, 'Why feel fear? Isn't it God's house? Far from scaring me, the infinite spaces accompany and move me so that my soul wants to fly through them with the trust of a child of God.'"[2] She was so used to the infinity of God, in which she so loved to immerse herself, that the beauty of earth was but a small reflection of the grandeur of God, which was her natural and familiar home.

Although she could easily go into the theoretical aspects of religion, Juanita was impatient with these and wanted to concentrate on the person of Christ. "She preferred to see God incarnate and acting in the sacred person of Christ," said Luis. "Juanita was in love with Christ."[3] However important the philosophical and dogmatic base of Christian theology is in underpinning faith, Juanita realized there was no point in trying to win her brother over by intellectual argument. Unless his heart was set on fire by the love of God that so consumed her, he would be unmoved by such arguments to make what has been described as that longest of journeys, from the head to the heart. What she tried to do was make him aware of the love for God which was so strong in her and trust that he would then know and experience for himself that God was not some remote deity "out there," but One who loved his children so much that he had come down to live among us, who died for us and was now living within those hearts who would accept his love.

The holiday was not wholly given up to these discussions. There were, as usual, their long horse treks and walks into the mountains, usually stopping at a shrine to Our Lady high up on the mountain. Juanita was also reading Saint Teresa of Avila's autobiography and making sure she did not neglect her prayer. It seems that there was no Mission that year, because Juanita noted that she hadn't been able to receive Communion for a month, a real hardship for her.

Everyone was interested in some excavations that were being carried out at the Indian cemetery in Chacabuco, and Juanita described them in great detail. "They've discovered beautifully painted pieces of pots and plates," she wrote to Carmen. "Even though they've been buried for a century, they are perfectly preserved, and one can see the progress they made, as there are some—the most primitive ones—that are made of mud. Others are of baked clay and painted in different colors. They've also discovered bullets and other pieces of artillery; the latter are quite large and heavy. And to think that they're only pebbles compared with those used in warfare nowadays."[4]

Juanita felt she could speak with some authority on military matters, because regiments were assembling in the area for military maneuvers to be carried out on 12 February. The regimental captain had already made himself known to the families around, and Juanita reported that he was providing a lot of entertainment for them, reciting poetry and singing songs, and described herself as well versed in the Battle of Chacabuco after the captain gave them a talk on it.

Two days before the start of the maneuvers they went for a trip to the Lourdes Shrine in Santiago and Juanita was overwhelmed by the experience. "At Lourdes we found heaven," she wrote lyrically in her diary.

> This word alone causes the deepest cords to vibrate in the Christian, the Catholic. Lourdes! Who doesn't feel moved when pronouncing that word! It means Heaven in this exile. The word bears under its mantle of mystery whatever great things the Catholic heart is capable of feeling. Her name causes past memories to be taken away and deeply touches the intimate feelings of our soul. It contains joy, superhuman peace, in which the pilgrim, fatigued by the sorrowful journey of life, can find rest; can without fear put down his baggage, which is our human miseries, and open his mouth to receive the water of consolation and comfort....

I didn't believe such happiness could exist on
earth; yesterday my heart, while thirsting for it, found
it. My soul was ecstatic at your virginal feet, listening
to you. You were speaking and your maternal language
was so tender. It was from heaven, almost divine." [5]

All too soon the holidays once again drew to a close and Juanita
was faced with "that terrible return to school on the 8th of March," as
she described it to Graciela.[6] It was her final year, and back at school
she was put in charge of some of the younger girls. It wasn't an easy
task. Just as, years before, her cousins and siblings had tried to provoke her, so the young girls in her charge did now. They actually had
immense respect and love for her, nicknaming her "mater amabilis,"
Mother Most Loving, a title of Our Lady by which she is specially
honored in Sacred Heart convents. The children admitted they tried to
wind Juanita up just because she was so easy and pleasant with them
and usually went along with the teasing. On one occasion, though,
she was too easygoing, allowing the girls to misbehave at table and
letting them go on talking, until she was told she should be stricter
with them. Juanita then became angry with the girls and told them
that they were being very disagreeable. It was quite a mild reproof,
but she immediately regretted her remarks. The reflections she made
on the event afterward show how level headed and clear-sighted she
was: "Would Jesus have acted in that way? Of course not! He would
have scolded them and would not have excused them, but he would
not have insulted them as I did. It's true that it took me a long time to
get control of myself, but afterward I spoke of my anger and the next
day to humble myself I begged forgiveness from the children."[7] No
wonder she remarked that each day she felt they loved her more.

On another occasion they began to tease her so much that she began
to cry. She had a headache and her back ached; she wasn't feeling at

all well and it was too much for her. However, they, too, showed they could make amends. At recess later, she had it out with them; they made up with her and sent her a holy picture as a peace offering.

Small events such as these, the stuff of school life with its ups and downs and its misunderstandings, were the material on which Juanita worked to become the saint that she knew Jesus was calling her to become. Her diary for this year was full of her struggles to overcome her pride, to try and remain united with Our Lord, to give him, with joy, her pain and her suffering and her struggles for the souls she longed to save.

In April Juanita was given as her director a Claretian priest, Father José Blanch, who was able to guide her firmly and wisely. She was obviously still having trouble with her feelings of anger, however rarely she showed it. For example, she recorded one occasion when sweets were handed round, and she threw her piece on the ground in a fit of pique because it was smaller than the others. His advice was never to manifest her anger exteriorly; to be lovable with the person who caused her anger, and to be silent, to put down the anger in her heart. He also assured her that she did indeed have a vocation to be a Carmelite, although he advised her not to speak too much to others about her vocation, except her mother and Mother Izquierdo, the Sister in charge of students. He gave her permission to do little acts of mortification; with her sweet tooth, one big sacrifice was to give up caramels sometimes. He also allowed her to renew her vow of virginity.

On 15 June, she received what was to her a crowning happiness—she was given the medal and blue ribbon of a Child of Mary, which was the highest honor the school could bestow on their star pupils. The "citation" was for those students who were "exemplary in their piety, in the fulfillment of their duties and for their excellent conduct." Juanita was so proud of this honour that from now on she always signed her letters with the initials H.M. (the Spanish for Child of Mary) after her name. For her, the award was a constant reminder to her to grow in ever closer likeness to Mary, whom she called her "mirror": "My mirror must be Mary. Given that I'm her daughter, I must resemble her and thus I must resemble Jesus." She goes on immediately to add, "I must love only Jesus. Hence my heart must hold the seal of God's love. My eyes must constantly attend to the voice of the Divine Crucified One."[8] Her great love for Mary, far from detracting from Jesus, quite rightly drew her to an ever more intense love of Jesus. Going to Mary, she always heard Mary's words, "Do whatever he tells you."[9]

Since Juanita had now received confirmation from her confessor that she did indeed have a Carmelite vocation, she now began to take positive steps towards her goal. One of her friends, Graciela, had a sister in the Carmel of Los Andes. She now told Chela, as she was nicknamed, of her strong attraction to becoming a Carmelite, and asked her if she could obtain a copy of the Carmelite Rule for her. To her great delight, Chela shared a letter from her Carmelite sister with her. "This is the first time I received anything from a Carmelite. What a delightful beginning," she wrote to Chela.[10] She had probably forgotten about the little holy picture card she'd received a few years earlier from the Prioress of the Santiago Monastery on Carmel Street. Juanita never seems to have approached this Carmel for information or with the possibility of entering there. It was closer to her home, but for this reason she might have avoided contacting them in case news of her vocation got around, something she didn't want to happen at this point. In addition, it was a well-appointed monastery, and Juanita was seeking something poorer. It did not attract her.

Nothing happened about the Los Andes Carmel until August, when Chela went to visit her sister. She showed the notebooks in which Juanita had written letters to her to Sister Teresita, who remembered that she had actually held Juanita in her arms when she was a baby. Teresita and the Prioress, Mother Angelica, asked Chela lots of questions about Juanita and suggested she write to them. Mother Angelica sent her a Carmelite scapular medal.

Juanita wrote her first letter to her future Prioress on 5 September. She had heard from Father Colom on 22 August that there had been elections as the Monastery, in which Mother Angelica had been elected for another term. It wasn't possible to write from school, but towards the end of August she became so ill, suffering from extreme exhaustion, headaches, back pains, and severe chest pains, that on 1 September she was sent home to recuperate. Juanita told Mother Angelica of the problems she was having, especially regarding her poor health. "Nevertheless, I've turned all this over to the Most Holy Virgin," she added, "and I believe she's going to open the doors of that blessed refuge, if it is God's will."[11]

In a letter to Chela earlier that year she wrote that two points of the Carmelite vocation are prayer and mortification, and these were the two points she now raised with the Prioress.

Earlier that year she had been reading Elizabeth of the Trinity intensively. The notes she made show her remarkable ability to assimilate and summarize the teachings of the young nun, who had died when Juanita was six years old. She found in Elizabeth a kindred soul. "She enchants me. Her soul is like mine," Juanita wrote in her diary. "Though she was a saint I'll imitate her and become a saint. I want to live with Jesus in the depths of my soul."[12] She, too, would then find her heaven on earth, for where Jesus is, there is heaven. This was a phrase she often repeated, because it so perfectly reflected her own experience. In her diary notes, she echoed Elizabeth's beautiful Prayer to the Trinity that this intimate union is accomplished by fulfilling his will joyfully at every moment. "Nothing must disturb me. All must be peace, like the peace that inundates the angels in heaven. By living in silence, because in this way the Holy Spirit will draw forth from me harmonious sounds and the Father, together with the Spirit, will form the image of the Word in me."[13]

"How I long to give myself over to prayer, to live constantly united to our Lord!" she now wrote to Mother Angelica. "Now I'm trying to recollect myself in spirit. There I adore, console and love my Jesus."[14]

Juanita also acknowledged that if she went to Carmel it would be to suffer, but that suffering was not unknown to her. "In it I find my joy, for Jesus is on the cross and He is love. And what does suffering matter if a person loves? The life of a Carmelite is one of suffering, loving and praying, and I find my whole ideal in this. My Jesus has taught me these three things since I was a little girl."[15]

It was a hard time for her. The school had a retreat in August, but even then her illness prevented her from going to Mass and receiving Communion. Communion gave her not only spiritual strength but bodily strength, too, so to be deprived of it was a great sacrifice. She tried to make a spiritual communion and to meditate, but her lethargy made it almost impossible. Was it really feasible to think she would be strong enough to live the rigors of the Carmelite life? Juanita brought the matter up once again with her confessor. He assured her once again that she did indeed have a Carmelite vocation. But was it a long term one? He suggested it could be short term, a transitory or momentary vocation to free her "from all evil in body or soul."[16] He suggested she could also be a Carmelite spiritually, following a Carmelite way of life at home, structuring her days to a similar pattern. Juanita didn't record what she thought of this. She would know that Elizabeth of the Trinity, facing similar problems, said that if she was unable to enter Carmel she would be a "Carmelite in the world." Nevertheless, both longed for the cloister.

In her diary for 2 October Juanita actually wrote that she was happy to be back in school again after the September vacations. During the vacations they had gone by train to Bellavista, and then on to the estate of Don Ricardo to join a house party. They traveled by car, which was a new and exciting experience for them. Don Ricardo celebrated Independence Day with hot air balloons, fireworks and donkey rides. On 26 September they went to the School of Aviation and saw Chiro, her future brother-in-law, fly an airplane. Her one disappointment was that her father was in San Javier on business and couldn't be with them.

Nevertheless, she was glad to be back at school. One of the benefits, perhaps the supreme one for her, was that at school she was under the same roof as the Blessed Sacrament. Not only could she go daily to Mass, her health permitting, but at each moment her thoughts could fly to the tabernacle where her Lord was. Not that she was enjoying her previous ease in prayer; quite the contrary:

> "It's been a long time since I've known what fervor is. I hear the voice of Jesus, but I don't see him," she wrote: "I don't feel his love. I'm cold, insensible; but this helps me to see my own nothingness and my misery. Thus it is that, when I'm with Jesus, I don't speak to him, because my imagination flies to other things. But when I return to myself I cry when I see how ungrateful I am with my dear Jesus, since he comes to dwell in my soul which is so filled with misery and I scarcely speak with him. In the end, I offer myself entirely to Jesus. I want to lose my nothingness in the abyss of his infinite love and power"[17]

"I don't know what is happening to me," Juanita wrote in bewilderment. She wanted to mortify herself, even wear a hair shirt, and yet she admitted in her diary that she had an unusual craving for her favorite caramels. "Today I had such a hunger that I ate all those I could and the ones that tasted best. It pains me to see that this is the way I am."[18] She longed to be detached from worldly things, yet took pleasure in how she looked. She wanted to pray, to turn her thoughts to the Lord, but found her prayer dry and without fervor. "I've been very strange," she wrote on 9 October. "I had a strong desire to behave badly, to become angry, finally, to the point of crying."[19]

At the beginning of the retreat Juanita made in August, she heard the voice of Jesus tell her that they were going together into solitude, and that he would search through his little house to see what was lacking, so that he could purify it. She was now going through this process of purification, and it was making her stronger. At one time her confessor had asked how she would cope with dryness in prayer when she was in Carmel, when her whole purpose in life would be prayer. The thought had troubled her, but by now she knew the answer. She knew she loved Jesus, even when the going was hard, and that she belonged to him. That was all that mattered:

> Jesus, give me the cross, but give me the strength to carry it. It matters not whether You give me the abandonment of Calvary or the joys of Nazareth. I only want to see You contented. It doesn't bother me to be unable to feel, to be insensible as a rock, because I know, my sweet Jesus, that You know I love You. Give me the cross. I want to suffer for You; but teach me to suffer by loving, with joy and with humility.

> Lord, if it please You that the darkness of my soul become deeper, that I not see You, it will not bother me because I want to fulfill Your will.[20]

Juanita's desire for Carmel was as strong as ever, apart from a wobble on 18 October, when her weariness, which had now been diagnosed as anemia, tempted her to feel that her vocation was an illusion. It upset her that Mother Izquierdo was increasingly coming to the view that she did not have a vocation or the health to become a Carmelite. However, talking about it to her confessor a few days later, the priest told her that it was for him to pronounce on the subject, not a religious.

But she had further worries about her vocation. To enter Carmel she needed to bring with her a dowry, but with her father's lack of education and experience in business affairs the family financial situation was getting worse and worse, and she was worried about their straitened circumstances. Earlier that year they had had to move from their stately mansion on San Domingo Street to a house in Vergara Street. When she asked her father for some money she needed, his reply was that he didn't have any. She was now worried that her father might not be able to afford the dowry for her. In addition, Juanita noticed that he had a marked hostility against the Carmelite nuns and she was worried that he would refuse his consent once she told him of her intentions.

As far as Juanita was concerned, she could accept their relative poverty with equanimity for she was, after all, intending to live a life of poverty in Carmel. She had always had an enormous generosity and love for the poor: "Juanita's charity was without limit toward the poor who visited our home," Luis testified. "I saw her waiting on them with her own hands hundreds of times, taking them food and clothing with a loving smile."[21] When on holiday she would take medicine to the tenant farmers on their property or to the sick people in the town, caring for their needs herself. She did it all with an unobtrusive naturalness and grace so that it didn't seem as if she were dispensing charity to them. There was one little orphaned boy, called Juanito, whom she had "adopted." She reserved money from her savings and her pocket money so that she could buy things for him. "I collected 30 pesos on my feast day," she noted in her diary. "I'm going to buy shoes for Juanito, and the rest I'll give to my mother to hold for me so it will given to the poor. It is so rich to give to the poor. I gave my shoes to Juanito's nurse."[22] She also pawned her watch to raise funds for him, and anxiously asked after him when she entered Carmel. Sadly, though, he was so upset by her disappearance that he ran away.

That was not her only worry. Someone told Juanita that she would have to wait two years after leaving school before she would be allowed to enter Carmel. If that were so, then she would ask her parents to take her out of school early. She wrote anxiously to Mother Angelica who was able to assure her that this, thankfully, was not the case.

During a time of prayer on 16 November, the Lord assured her that she would indeed enter Carmel and encouraged her in the difficult path she was treading:

> Last night I spent one hour with Jesus. We were speaking intimately. He reproached me because in my pains and doubts I didn't have recourse to His Heart as I used to. He desires that I be a virgin, without being touched by any creatures, because I must belong entirely to Him. I rested myself on His Heart. Then He spoke to me about poverty. I came away from Him without a thing. Everything belongs to Him. Everything passes away and is vanity. Afterwards He spoke to me about humility of thought, action and empty knowledge. Finally, He opened his Heart to me and showed me that because of my prayers He had written the name of my father there. He told me I should resign myself to not seeing the fruit of my prayers, but that I would obtain everything. Afterwards He manifested His love to me,

but in such a way that I began to cry. He showed me His greatness and my nothingness, and told me He had chosen me as a victim. I must climb Calvary with Him. Together we should undertake the conquest of souls: He the Captain, and I the soldier. Our motto, the cross. Our cry love. He told me I should suffer with joy and with love, and every day I should remove a thorn from His heart. He told me that I should love Him and that I will be a Carmelite; that I should not be discouraged; that I should not talk about this, since they'll try to dissuade me from my vocation. And finally, that I should belong to Him alone: a virgin, intact and pure.[23]

Juanita said that Jesus had chosen her as a "victim," a term that Saint Thérèse of Lisieux had first used of her own path. This is a very precise term. Jesus said that all Christians must take up their cross and follow him, and self denial is part of the Christian way of life. But of some he asks a closer conformity to him in his passion, a deeper sharing in his cross. This is what he was asking of Juanita, and her spiritual and physical suffering at this time was a process of purification to fit her for this special calling.

What God willed for her he was giving her a desire for, and despite her ill health, which caused her a lot of pain, she was eager to embrace suffering, if this was the will of God for her. She asked her confessor for permission to undertake various acts of mortification, such as praying with her arms in the form of a cross, fasting, wearing a hair shirt. She even tried putting stones in her shoe but quickly abandoned it as her difficulty in walking would have been noticeable to others. What she did she wanted to do for God alone.

Juanita realized, though, that the most effective forms of mortification were the little things of everyday life— putting herself out for others, being at their service, not drawing attention to herself, biting back the angry word.

The universal testimony to Juanita was that her interior trials were known to very few. Her joyful acceptance of them meant that she never became morbid. There was a natural reserve in her, but her friends said that she stood out at school for her friendliness and sweetness. As Juanita herself said, she was happy everywhere since, after all, God was everywhere. God's grace was being perfected in her, and the result was a well-rounded human being, natural, warm-hearted and loving. Luis said that she was a stupendous friend, easy to get along with and discreet. At school, she was always ready to help the poorest pupils or those who had difficulties with their studies. Her unobtrusive self-denial and self-control had given her a commanding presence that made her stand out in any group, however much she tried to stay in the background. She was, said Luis, an irresistible magnet.

Notes

1. *Diary* 18
2. *Testimonies*, p. 73
3. *Testimonies*, p. 68
4. *Letter* 10
5. *Diary* 19
6. *Letter* 11
7. *Diary* 22
8 *Diary* 15
9. Jn 2:5
10. *Letter* 13
11 *Letter* 14
12. *Diary* 28
13. Ibid.
14. *Letter* 14
15. Ibid.
16. *Diary* 33

17. *Diary* 34
18. Ibid.
19. Ibid.
20. Ibid.
21. *Testimonies*, p. 76
22. *Diary* 26
23. *Diary* 37

Chapter 7
Dear Old Algarrobo

Despite her poor health and her time off from school, Juanita did win prizes at the end of term, as did Rebecca; Luis, too, took all the honors in his class at school. Before the term ended, Juanita joined in an All Saints Eve Recreation Day where the Children of Mary took over the manual work of the lay sisters in the school, which delighted her. Two days before, a procession was held in honour of the Infant of Prague, to pray for a cure for Juanita's youngest brother Ignatio, who had injured his leg in an accident. There was no cure as yet for him, although there was a gradual improvement. The real joy for Juanita was that her father was there and took part in the procession. Being away so much in the country, overseeing the family estates, he had grown lax in the practice of his faith, and for over a year hadn't been to Mass or confession. She was worried about his spiritual health, which she said was worse than Ignacio's physical health. How encouraged she would have been, then, by Jesus's assurance that he had written the name of her father on his Heart.

Two days after the term ended, the family went to a gymnastic parade at the Military School, and a riding school display; then on Christmas Day they went along the Alameda, where stalls had been set up in aid of poor children. Juanita remarked that "it was real robbery, since they were asking 20 or 30 pesos for everything."[1]

There were doubts as to whether the family could afford a holiday that year. They couldn't afford to rent a house in Chacabuco, but they were, after all, able to go on holiday to Algarrobo, a seaside town seventy miles from Santiago. The one thing that spoiled her happiness was that her father wasn't with them. "Why don't you try to get here, even if it's just for a few days?" she wrote to him plaintively. "You don't know how bad I feel when I see the other girls so happy with their fathers. Come, please, because we have the joy of being so seldom with you during the year."[2] Her father hadn't even been with them over Christmas. He was perhaps glad to have the excuse of having to oversee their dwindling estates and not to be at home so that he did not have to face his wife. Don Miguel was a gentle character, and acutely aware of how badly he was letting down his family with his business failures, which were depleting his wife's inheritance. She had a punctilious and demanding character, and it was easier for him to be out of the way rather than face her reproaches. From Doña Lucia's point of view, she must have been thoroughly frustrated at the way their finances were draining away.

In the meantime, they were enjoying their holiday in Algarrobo, despite their father's absence. At that time it was a very poor town, the houses piles of bricks and beamed roofs. The house the family rented was not nearly as luxurious as those they had been accustomed to, but it was right on the beach, and its poverty was more than compensated for by the wonderful views and an enchanting coastline. They were joined by a large circle of friends and enjoyed their favorite activities—the bathing was ideal, there were wonderful walks in the surrounding countryside and, of course, horseback riding further inland, with routes passing huge waterfalls and through tree covered mountains. "You couldn't imagine anything more beautiful," she wrote to Carmen, "because it makes me think of the God who created such a beautiful earth, even if it is a place of sorrow. What can heaven be like, I often ask myself, when it's about enjoyment?"[3] The shifting colors of the ocean as it reflected the passing clouds enthralled her. "Carmen, does it ever happen to you that when you're looking at the ocean you feel a longing for the infinite? We feel in our soul an inexplicable loneliness that only God can fill, because everything seems so small."[4] The place of sorrow she spoke of could be seen in the poverty of the people in the village, and as always, Juanita was generous with what money was available to her in giving to the poor. But of even greater concern to her was their spiritual poverty, so she set about organizing her friends to run a catechism class. They also set up a musical choir for the Masses and Benediction, although they were hampered by a lack of accompaniment.

She was also reading the Autobiography of Saint Teresa of Avila again, and enjoying *The Life of the Princess*, a biography of Princess Louise, daughter of Louis XV of France, who became a Carmelite nun. Juanita was glad of the quiet periods she could snatch between the many outings with her friends. She admitted to Carmen that some of the girls in the social circle at Algarrobo were not her type. There were some of her close friends there, Herminia and Marta among them, who were on the same wavelength as she. While thoroughly enjoying themselves, and, like her, living life to the full, some of them were considering a religious vocation or a life of faith and charitable works in the world, and were not drawn to the more frivolous aspects of the holidays and the inevitable match-making.

Another of her friends there was Luz Rivas de Freire, who lived nearby, and it was the social gatherings at the de Rivas' home that were not to her taste. "From everything I saw and heard, I've got a very poor impression of their social events," she confided to Carmen. "I ask myself how they can call that kind of entertainment where nothing goes on but pure foolishness."[5] Juanita knew she had to take part in such gatherings, but she unobtrusively distanced herself from the more objectionable aspects of them. She took her vow of virginity seriously and made sure that her friendships with the young men in the circle never went beyond friendly camaraderie. She never wore low-cut dresses, and unless her mother ordered her to dress up more, didn't wear jewelry. At dances, she got out of joining in the dancing by playing for them instead at the piano or on the guitar, all with such grace that no one realized her motives.

She much preferred running the catechism classes. It wasn't an easy task, as the children were very unruly and undisciplined, some with alcoholic parents, and it took all her patience and good humor. One ploy was to give them plenty of activity, organizing games and competitions for them such as sack races and donkey races, which would use up some of their energy, as well as giving them lots of fun. Juanita threw herself energetically into these activities, too, happily ending up covered with dirt and enjoying every minute. She would also take her guitar along and strike up lively Chilean songs for them in her beautiful alto voice.

However much she tried to be unobtrusive, her genuine goodness could not be hidden. The Freire de Rivas were non-religious free-thinkers, but even so they were drawn to that evident quality of holiness within her. Luz's mother, Julia, often had discussions with Juanita about the writings of Saint Teresa of Avila and Saint John of the Cross. Julia remained a non-believer, but remarked, "You people don't know what a treasure getting to know that girl has been for me."[6]

The holiday did the whole family good. Little Ignacio's leg was getting stronger; he was putting on weight, and became tanned and fit. Just before they went on holiday Lucia had been taken ill with a high fever, but was now recovered. However, she was unhappy to be separated from Chiro, who had gone away to Valparaiso, and worried whether the family's financial situation would delay their marriage. Her mother, too, was feeling better after a few bouts of weakness. Juanita still suffered from lassitude due to her anemia, with headaches, chest pains and nausea, but was grateful for the quiet periods, away from all the activity, that these allowed her. Rebecca, of course, had thoroughly enjoyed the social round, which suited her love of partying.

They left "dear old Algarrobo" on 12 March, all in floods of tears. The return to school was softened by the unexpected arrival home of their father the same day, so Juanita and Rebecca were allowed a couple of days off from school to be with him. However, changes were happening at home, and Juanita's school days were soon to draw to an end.

Notes

1. *Letter* 17
2. *Letter* 21
3. *Letter* 19
4. Ibid.
5. *Letter* 21
6. *Testimonies*, p. 71

Chapter 8
Last Days at School

The Sacred Heart College on Maestranza Street was recognized as a teacher training school if students completed the last two years of college, leaving at age 19. Since Juanita did not intend to become a teacher, it was decided she should leave at the end of the school year, in July. In addition, any problems over Lucia and Chiro's marriage had been sorted out, and a date for the wedding was set for mid-June. Once Lucia was married, her mother wanted Juanita to take Lucia's place in running the household.

Her last months at the school were very hard. Juanita's spiritual darkness intensified, even to the point where she doubted the existence of God. She was hampered in coping with this because her official confessor, Fr. Blanch, was no longer in Santiago, and she had to correspond with him by letter. She was reluctant to go to someone else and start all over again with another priest, and she was hoping all the time that Fr. Blanch would be sent back to Santiago. The advantage, as far as we are concerned, is that her letters to him were preserved, and they give us an insight into this period of purification.

"I have many doubts about my Carmelite vocation," she wrote to him. These doubts were her ongoing ones of her poor health and her conviction that her father would oppose her vocation. "Doubts, too, about faith, so that sometimes I ask myself if God exists, Rev. Father, as I felt so abandoned by him. I looked at my crucifix and it all seemed like a trick of my mind. I cried and begged the Virgin's help, but she didn't help me, either. At last Our Lord took pity on me and allowed me to hear his voice in my heart. Then it was all over and I was filled with peace."[1]

These periods of peace, though, were few. Mostly her normal state of soul was one of terrible dryness. Although Juanita didn't stop going to daily Mass, to her distress she was often distracted at Communion time and felt none of her former fervor. "I don't feel like going to Communion," she wrote to Mother Angelica, "because I say to myself: what, do you think Jesus wants you to receive him in Communion with your soul as hard as a rock? Still, a love that is not felt that lives in the deepest part of my soul makes me go up to receive my Jesus."[2]

She was advised to use vocal prayer with short, ten-minute sessions instead of long stretches. This advice would suit a beginner in prayer, but in Juanita's case this advice was not the best. Despite her youth, she was now far more advanced in prayer than that. The reality was that God was leading her into a deeper form of prayer. The works of Saint John of the Cross, which she had already started to read, would prove a much better guide for her, since her dryness was a mystical "dark night." Our Lord was leading Juanita into a more passive form of prayer in which, as Saint John of the Cross said, "an individual does nothing, for God accomplishes the work in him, while he acts as the recipient."[3] Vocal prayer or an attempt to any form of discursive meditation at this point would do more harm than good.

Saint John explained that this dryness was of God since "the memory ordinarily turns to God solicitously and with painful care, and the soul thinks it is not serving God but turning back, because it is aware of this distaste for the things of God. Hence, it is obvious that this aversion and dryness is not the fruit of laxity and tepidity, for a lukewarm person does not care much for the things of God nor is he inwardly solicitous about them."[4]

The reason for the dryness was that God was, in Saint John's terminology, transferring his goods from the sense to the spirit, bringing Juanita from meditation to contemplation, where she no longer had the power to work at prayer or meditate with her faculties on the things of God. The result was just as Saint John of the Cross described—worry lest she was going astray, distress, doubts and fear that God had abandoned her. But all that God was asking of her was patience and perseverance while he accomplished his work in her.

Juanita herself tried to accept this trial generously and joyfully, since she had asked Christ to deprive her of all consolation so that other souls could encounter the peace and joy in the sacraments and in prayer that she had known for herself. It became, therefore, a form of intercession for others besides being a trial of faith given her by God. She embraced it as something she could offer up for souls; and above all, for her father, Miguel, and Luis, to return to the faith.

When Saint John of the Cross composed his work on the Dark Night, he was imprisoned in one of his monasteries and undergoing great suffering. The "dark night" of prayer is often accompanied by exterior trials as well. For Juanita, these were problems within her family and at school, as well as her ill health.

Miguel was causing the whole family a great deal of worry. He was very gifted, an accomplished poet, and this led him into a Bohemian style of life and heavy drinking. He had completed his period of military service, and the previous September Chiro had tried to get him a job. However, his wild way of life was driving his mother to distraction and frequent arguments and confrontations ensued. Juanita had much more sympathy for him, and with her gentleness and sense of fair play, tried to make excuses for him and play the peacemaker.

There were more problems at school. Mother Izquierdo, who had until now given unfailing guidance to her, seemed to turn against Juanita in her last months at school. Not that the nun had ever been soft with her; surely discerning Juanita's exceptional qualities and depth of character, she demanded a lot of her young pupil. "Do everything for the love of God, do not seek the consolations of God, but the God of consolations; live just for the day," was the advice she gave Juanita and which Juanita jotted down in her diary.[5]

Knowing how disciplined Juanita normally was, Mother Izquierdo was not impressed by her lack of control when a bee got into the classroom one day. Juanita bounded up and dashed out of the room, much to her humiliation, especially when the nun looked at her with such a "fixed and profound stare" that she wished the ground would swallow her up.

On another occasion, it seems that Juanita had had to speak out about one of the Sisters to prevent her from giving a bad example. This had caused quite a bit of gossip among the girls. She was convinced that Mother Izquierdo would think her a liar, but her sense of responsibility gave her no other option.

She was distressed and bewildered at Mother Izquierdo's attitude toward her as her time at school drew to a close. "I don't know what I've done," she wrote in her diary:

> She's not the same mother towards me that she used to be. I continue to have the same affection and trust toward her. This frightens my soul. Why, my Jesus, are you placing this coldness round my poor heart? It is because you love me. You want to encircle me only with your love so I will not be attached to any creature. This helps me to see that love doesn't exist on earth, but in God alone; because, if favored, chosen and holy souls forget or are indifferent, what will other people be like? You, Jesus, are the only One capable of inspiring me to fall in love ... My Jesus, be the Jesus of Bethany for me.[6]

One can only guess at Mother Izquierdo's motives, but if Juanita recognized that Jesus was detaching her from a dearly loved Mother and guide, then it could be that Jesus was also detaching Mother Iz-quierdo, herself a deeply respected and holy nun, from a dearly loved pupil. She would have been less than human if she hadn't entertained the hope that such an outstanding pupil would enter her own Order rather than the Carmelites. Was that why Fr. Blanch had told Juanita not to take notice when Mother Izquierdo told her that she did not have a Carmelite vocation? Mother Izquierdo was aware of the depth of love Juanita had for Jesus. One day, when Juanita was having doubts as to whether the voice who still spoke to her in her darkness really was Jesus, she asked for a "sign"—that the nun would ask her: "Do you love Our Lord?" "How moved I was today," [7] she related, "when I heard Mother say to me: 'Do you love Christ?' I blushed with emotion and became silent. She said to me: 'Are you not answering with all your soul?' I replied: 'It would be monstrous if I did not love him.'... Oh, Jesus, your love annihilates and confounds me!"[8]

A few days afterwards, Juanita developed a very painful tooth. When the dentist tried to extract one of her teeth it split, causing her so much pain that she nearly went out of her mind. She had to suffer the pain, offering it all to God, for another two weeks until it was extracted under chloroform.

Before leaving school Juanita made a retreat, entering into it with the theme, "Speak, Lord, for Your servant is listening." (1 Samuel 3:9) Her one goal in life was to love and serve God, "For if I love God, I'll fulfill His divine will. What is His will? That I follow Him and be perfect. How can I most easily attain perfection? By means of the evangelical counsels: obedience, chastity and poverty. I must follow Jesus Christ wherever He calls me, since that is my salvation."[9]

At the center of her life was the Eucharist. Here she met Jesus, whom she loved with all her heart. The realization that Jesus Himself, not a relic, a memento or an outward symbol, was present there, affected her profoundly:

> When they speak of the Eucharist I feel something so strange in myself that I'm unable to think or do anything. It's as though I'm paralyzed and I believe that if in an instant there came to me impulses of love I'd be unable to resist them. My Jesus, I annihilate myself before Your love! You, God of heaven and earth, of the seas, of the mountains, of the star studded firmament; You, Lord, who are adored by the angels in an ecstasy of love; You, Jesus in Your humanity; You, the living bread!"[10]

These were heavenly days for her, a break in her dryness, when she had more time to spend in prayer. Jesus again reassured her about her vocation and buoyed her up as her school days drew to an end. So many times she had spoken of how "terrible" the school was, how she would like it to burn down, how she went cold at the thought of returning to it after the summer holidays. But now that she was due to leave it forever, with its opportunities for visiting Jesus in the Blessed Sacrament, with its depth of studies, with its opportunities to receive communion daily, she realized how much these years had meant to her. She would miss the many friends she had made there. She would even miss the structured life that she had originally found so constricting and cold. Above all, she would miss the sisters—or most of them; one sister, Mother du Bose, unfailingly made her blood boil, she said—especially Mother Izquierdo and Mother Rios, who had been such strong, wise and dearly loved guides to her in her spiritual journey.

She felt apprehensive of the new life that was opening out before her, with the ties that bound her to school life being severed. It was hard for her to be present for the opening of the new term, knowing that she now had none of her previous responsibilities and duties in the school.

She resolved not to cry as she said goodbye to everyone, however much she felt like it. "I haven't cried," she confided to her diary, "but my heart is torn to pieces."[11] She had resolved to keep serene and not cry, even though it might mean the nuns would think she was indifferent, and offered it up for her father and brothers to return to the practice of their faith. Above all, it was a preparation she knew she would have to make over the next few months, for that final separation of her entry into Carmel.

Notes

1. *Letter* 29
2. *Letter* 30
3. *The Ascent of Mount Carmel* 13:1
4. *The Dark Night* 9:3
5. Cf. *Diary* 31
6. *Diary* 40
7. July 17
8. *Diary* 41
9. *Diary* 42
10. Ibid.
11. *Diary* 43

Chapter 9
Life at Home

A short while before she left school Juanita had a talk with the Mother Vicar of the Sacred Heart Sisters who gave her some valuable guidance for the way ahead and which she noted down in her diary:

> I should be a guardian angel for the family. Every day I should get up for Mass and make my meditation. I should remember that I'm a Child of Mary. I should imitate her, be humble, put up with humiliations. I shouldn't allow myself to be carried away by impressions, but always preserve a serene countenance, despite contradictions and sorrows. I should be very affectionate with my mother, and now the time has come to thank her not only with words but with deeds for all she has done for me. I'm going to spare her pain, console and help her in every way. I must be very affectionate with my father, be an angel and offer counsel to my brothers and sisters, and be so virtuous and mortified as to make virtue attractive to all. I should study, because today more than ever a woman must be informed. Finally, she told me that I will always retain the affection of the Sisters and that I can count on their prayers and sacrifices.[1]

At the end of the retreat she made before leaving school she added resolutions of her own:

> 1. I'll never miss my meditation, my Communion and Mass.
>
> 2. I'll make my particular examination of conscience and recite my morning and evening prayers on my knees.

3. I'll make my spiritual reading and preserve recollection in my soul, for it will keep me united with
Jesus and completely separate from the world.

4. I'll maintain a good character. I'll never allow myself to be governed by feelings or by my heart, but by
reason and by conscience.

5. I'll joyfully fulfill the will of God in sadness and
in joy, without ever betraying on my face what's going
on in my heart. I'll never cry, ever keeping in mind
the words of Saint Teresa: "It's imperative to have the
heart of a man and not that of a woman."

6. I'll never allow myself to be carried away by human respect, whether in my manner of conducting myself or in my words.[2]

Rather than aspirations and resolutions, these notes paint a true
picture of her life at home. Juanita had already worked out a timetable
for herself. She got up at 5:30 and meditated from 6 to 7. At 11:30
she made her examination of conscience. At midday she did spiritual
reading, with one hour of prayer in the evening.

Although Lucia and Chiro were married, they still lived at home;
Juanita took Lucia's place in running the household. It was something
she enjoyed, and, in a positively non-politically correct way, saw it as
a woman's role. "There's nothing more wonderful than to see a young
girl concerned with things of the house," she wrote to her father, "a
worker, having no other thought than to please those around her in
every way she can. I'm learning these things now. If, later on, God
wants me to have a household, I'll know how to fulfill all my duties."[3]
If God wanted her to have a household ... was this a subtle hint to her
father, perhaps, of other intentions, since she had still not told him of
her desire to enter Carmel?

Juanita valued home life so much because she considered there was no greater role in life than bringing up the next generation, and that a good education was essential to this: "The education of a woman is more important than that of a man, for she will form the man,"[4] she wrote. Her calling to Carmel was by no means because she did not value marriage and family life.

Being at home gave her even greater opportunities to help the poor people who came to their door. Wherever she was, whether at home, on their estates, or on holiday, she would often slip away to visit employees and their families, and visit the families of the children she was teaching in her catechism classes, taking them food, clothing and medicine. Any poor person coming to the house had a warm welcome. No one went away empty handed. Luis said that he saw her waiting on them herself hundreds of times. "Sometimes she broke away from the family quarters and went up to the third patio where the employees lived," he recalled. "There she would invent ways to help them with so much naturalness and grace that the employees didn't notice."[5] Their physical needs were as important to her as their spiritual needs; neither could be neglected. Luis remembered her asking him for socks and underwear for her little "adopted" orphan Juanito, feeding him and clothing him, as well as teaching him his faith and praying for him. To her, he was a symbol of all the poor and underprivileged children in the world. She couldn't help them all personally, but did what she could where she was and with the resources available to her.

Luis called her the guardian angel of her family. With her tact and good humor, she was a much better arbitrator in family affairs than her mother. She often had to intervene between Miguel and her mother, urging her to be more gentle and understanding in her approach toward him. Miguel would take himself off for weeks on end and then have to face his mother's wrath when he came back. He knew he was the odd

one out at home, the black sheep of the family, and only Juanita sought
to understand and empathize with him. As Miguel himself remarked,
"I don't fit in very well at home, but as for her, she's a real saint."
Rebecca, too, needed careful handling. She missed Juanita's
presence at school and she was becoming increasingly upset as the
inevitability of Juanita entering Carmel drew ever nearer. Juanita
wrote to Elena, a friend of hers still at school, and asked her to be a
confidante for Rebecca now that she was no longer there. Elena herself
was considering a religious vocation, and entered the Sacred Heart
Sisters three years later.

Juanita dearly loved her younger sister with her sunny disposition
and expansive character, nicknaming her "Negrita," because Rebecca
had a much darker complexion than herself. Her flighty ways sometimes caused Juanita pain, and Luis recalled an incident when Rebecca
did something shocking and in poor taste. Juanita chased after her as
Rebecca ran off, but when she caught up with her Juanita restrained
herself, gave her sister a big hug and forgave her. Understandably,
her brothers and sisters preferred Juanita's way of correction to their
mother's confrontations and reproaches. Not that it was always easy, as
that incident shows. Juanita had strong feelings and reactions herself,
and only her constant self-discipline kept them under control.

There was a strong bond of love and affection between Juanita
and her mother. Having a deep faith herself, Lucia had a profound
respect for her daughter, discerning her very real holiness and appre-
ciating her exceptional qualities. That was one reason why Juanita,
early on, felt she could confide her religious vocation to her mother.
Being at home now, that bond grew even stronger, although it wasn't
always easy. Juanita said that her mother was constantly giving her
orders and scolding her if she didn't do things well, often for no good
reason. She remarked that it was serving her as a good preparation for

religious life. It cost her a great deal not to answer back, and she said that she sometimes felt herself revolting inside against her mother's unreasonableness. Still, it was a splinter of the cross that she desired so much, and all the time it was grounding her ever more deeply in humility and self-sacrifice.

Juanita also had the support of another friend whom she made the day after leaving school, a second cousin, Elisita Valdés Ossa. She, too, wanted to enter Carmel, and Juanita found in her a true friend who shared her tastes, her aspirations and her ideals. Elisita was facing great opposition from her family, and Juanita wrote to Mother Angelica asking for their prayers for her: "The poor little thing really needs those prayers, for she finds herself in an environment supremely hostile to her inclinations. They make her go out a lot, and so she has little time for her spiritual exercises. We two help each other to love and serve Our Lord as best we can, and our conversations are always either to stimulate each other on the road to perfection or to speak of Carmel where both of us want to go. How I long that the day would come soon when I can say: 'I'm a Carmelite!'"[6] Elisita was never able to fulfill that dream; instead, throughout her life she engaged in social and charitable works, and founded a Catechetical Home named after her.

Juanita sympathized with Elisita being obliged to follow a social round, for this was one aspect of life at home to which she was not looking forward. She enjoyed social activities, but with her delicate sense of prudence and integrity, and her vow of chastity, she tried to avoid situations that might compromise her. The family often had weekend parties and dances in their home; Juanita couldn't avoid them, so she continued her practice of offering to play the piano or the guitar for the gathering, and she was in great demand for her beautiful singing voice. With her physical grace and coordination she was also an excellent dancer, and had received dancing lessons from an instructor called Harold.

An incident convinced her that God was indeed watching over her. One evening a group of them went to the opera, but there was a dance in it that was immodest. Juanita kept her eyes down, regretting that she hadn't brought her rosary with her. In the interval she went outside for a breath of fresh air, and Luis, who was there with his girlfriend handed her a rosary he had just found. "How this loving Mother (Mary) protects me," she wrote to Mother Angelica. "Why shouldn't I love her with all my soul? Being protected by her, what should I fear?"[7]

In a letter to Mother Angelica of 7 September, Juanita formally requested that she enter the Los Andes Carmel, and that her entry should be early the following year, in 1919. "Rev. Mother, right now I plead with you to admit me to that little dovecote nest," she wrote. "I know that I'm not worthy, my dear Mother, of this great favor; but, believe me, I'll work my whole life long to become a great saint. Saint Teresa says that it's not pride to espouse such lofty desires; quite the contrary, this will lift the soul to the most sublime things. I know that I'm very imperfect; but I trust that, with Our Lord's help and the help of the Most Holy Virgin I can wear the Carmelite habit with honor."[8]

Mother Angelica wrote to her by return of post accepting her application, but of course she would first have to visit the monastery. Arranging a date proved a problem. Juanita had hoped a visit could be arranged for October, but that wasn't possible. After that, she had arranged to go with Elisita to her family's farm at Cunaco on 28 October to run a Mission, and would be there until the end of November. The visit would have to wait until the New Year.

Once again, the Mission, given by the Redemptorist Fathers, was highly successful: 1,300 Communions, 70 First Communions, baptisms, confirmations and weddings. Juanita treasured the fact that she could go to Communion every day until the Mission priests left. They acted as sacristans in the chapel on the estate, which gave them the opportunity to spend time before the Blessed Sacrament. Coming into the chapel one day, Father Felix Henlé found Juanita there in ecstasy, raised some twelve inches above the floor, her face burning and her eyes riveted on the tabernacle.

It was a joy for her to be with Elisita, sharing the same aspirations for Carmel without drawing too much attention to their desire for prayer and for Carmel. One sticky moment came when one of their friends, Maria Larrain Moreno, began to talk about her sister Lucha, who had helped found the Monastery of Valparaiso earlier that year. Maria herself entered there and, like Juanita, died young in 1925. The two of them had to conceal, even from Maria, that they had similar plans, and started to laugh, then broke into a song, which they sang all day. The three of them pretended they were in a religious community and already in Carmel.

There was an exuberance about Juanita's letters from Cunaco. "I've become famous for my fits of laughter," she wrote to Rebecca. "We've done nothing but kid around. Prepare yourself. We are the last ones at table with Pepe. We've told so many jokes and laughed so much that sometimes I can't eat. And the most tragic part of it was that the priest who said grace after the meal had to stop his prayer halfway through. He was unable to continue because of the laughter and because we infected him with our laughter."[9]

"I'm quite a Yankee girl," she told Rebecca, referring to the Americanisms that were creeping into the Chilean language from the Americans who ran copper mines near Eli's farm.

Another day they went through the pasturelands and came to a bank where they stopped to rest for a while and enjoy the wonderful scenery. They came through a field on their way back and Juanita accidentally stepped on a snake's nest. "I don't think a scream like mine has ever before come from the human mouth," she wrote to Rebecca. "I ran screaming desperately, until I ran into Don Pepe, who had been very much frightened by our screams. He helped us get through. I thought of you, who surely would have taken the snake and wrapped it round your arm. I may bring you some lizards when I leave, for here we're stepping on them all the time."[10]

Every morning, she said, Herminia came to wake her up with water, chairs, a blanket and everything she found along the way to throw it all at her on top of the bed, although she, too, teased Herminia in return.

They fooled around everywhere, even when they tried out a new "Ave Maria" they had composed. "We're very proud of our improvisation. When we sounded the highest note, it occurred to Herminia to cover her ears, because with our powerful voices, she thought she'd rupture her eardrums. When we saw the way Gordita was gesticulating, we began to laugh. Instead of notes, we let out pure laughter, and I couldn't play the note on the organ. How fortunate that the people didn't see us. Fortunately we were in the oratory, and the farmers were out in the shed."[11]

The high spirits continued on their outings. Laughing at themselves, they went out riding in the rain covered with blankets, and waded ankle deep in mud on their treks on foot.

All this was, of course, natural high spirits among a group of young girls; but their enjoyment of each other's company, of the beautiful scenery, the activities they shared, the swimming, the tennis, the horseback riding, were all enhanced and given a new dimension by the love of God that bound them together even more deeply than ordinary friendship.

Juanita described that divine love in a long and beautiful letter she wrote to her friend, Elena Gonzales, during the holidays. In it, she expressed in finite human words the love of God that possessed her, and which really is beyond words:

> Tell me, is there anything greater on earth than the eternal, immutable, all-powerful God searching out a soul on earth to make her His own bride and seeking a human heart to join to His own Divine Heart, and in love achieving the most complete fusion? Further yet, that God would come down to earth and live here in the Eucharist, dying for love of us? Think of the greatest love on earth, and what is it in comparison with the love of the Infinite God?[12]

Such a love transfigures the person who accepts that love and allows it to live within her: "Love is the fusion of two souls in one in order to bring about mutual perfection. How can there be a unity of soul more perfect than the unity God makes between Himself and our soul. The soul united to God is so divinized that it begins to will and work in the pattern of Jesus Christ. Is there in the world anything greater in the world than God? Is there anything greater than a soul divinized? Isn't this the highest grandeur to which a human being can aspire?"[13]

Juanita acknowledged that she used to believe it was impossible to fall in love with a God we cannot see or touch with our hands, although we can see him in his works:

> But today I can affirm with my hand over my heart that God completely makes up for that sacrifice. You feel that love so much and those caresses from Our Lord that it seems God is there by your side. I feel Him so intimately united to me, that I want nothing more, except the beatific vision in heaven. I feel I'm filled with God and then I hold Him close to my heart and ask Him to make me experience the perfections

of His love. There's no separation between us. Wherever I go, God is with me in my poor heart. That's the little house where I dwell; it's my heaven here on earth. I live with God; and despite being on walks we converse with each other without anyone being able to surprise us or interrupt us.[14]

Juanita contrasts this with the frailty and impermanence of human love, which she sees as inevitably fading into indifference. Nevertheless, she innocently reveals from her own experience that this need not necessarily be so. Her love for God, far from detracting from her love for her family, friends, and those to whom she went out in help and concern, increased her sensitivity and ability to respond in love. God cannot be hugged and touched. People can be, however, and such human expressions of love were very much part of her makeup. Her love of God only made her love for others wider and deeper.

As for married love, like Saint Paul Juanita saw it as a reflection and a sacrament of divine love. When we observe the human love between a man and a woman reach its fullness, we come to an understanding of the love within the Trinity itself and the love of Christ for his Church. Juanita was later to make the comparison between her own consecrated life and her sister Lucia's love for Chiro that illustrated what Saint Paul was saying: "I've given him everything, it's true, but I've also come to possess the One who is Everything," she wrote to Lucia. "If Chiro's love and all his sacrifices for you make you love him more, what can I tell you, when in God love knows no limit and His immolation of self can never be greater since His Wisdom has exhausted every possibility?"[15] The key is the priority we give to that human love. It is a question of seeking first the kingdom of God. As Juanita put it, "Above all other beings, we should love and serve the Creator. Only then do human beings become the second expression of love."[16]

Notes

1. *Diary* 41
2. *Diary* 43
3. *Letter* 35
4. *Letter* 40
5. *Testimonies*, p. 76
6. *Letter* 37
7. Ibid.
8. *Letter* 36
9. *Letter* 43
10. Ibid.
11. Ibid.
12. *Letter* 40
13. Ibid.
14. Ibid.
15. *Letter* 112
16. *Letter* 40

Chapter 10
Los Andes Carmel

The family returned to Santiago in mid-December, and came down with influenza. Then, when Rebecca came home from school, Juanita had to go out to more social events in the period before Christmas. They saw the New Year in, joining the crowds on the Alameda. Juanita was almost overwhelmed by a mixture of joy and grief: joy at the thought that this time next year she would totally belong to the Lord in Carmel, and grief that this would be the last New Year she would spend at home with her family.

Juanita's dryness in prayer had eased somewhat, and for periods at a time she remained so immersed in God that she was oblivious to everything else. But a new problem surfaced. The previous year she had a passing conflict as to which Order she should enter—the Carmelites or the Sacred Heart nuns. Now this conflict returned with even greater force.

In her letter to Elena, Juanita listed the reasons why she preferred Carmel above other, active orders. Carmelites live in retirement from the world and are concerned with God alone. Their purpose is to become one with God, which is heaven. She preferred a more austere convent: "I find if you're going to become a nun, you shouldn't do it by halves." In Carmel one lives in continuous prayer; that is, in permanent touch with God. "The Carmelite purpose fills me with enthusiasm: to pray for sinners, to spend one's whole life sacrificing oneself, never seeing the fruits of prayer and sacrifice and yet united with God so that, in this way, His redeeming Blood circulates in her, and in the Church, in its members, so that they become holy."[1]

It is obvious from this that Juanita's desire to live retired from the world was far from being a selfish aspiration, concerned only with her own sanctification. The Carmelite vocation of prayer has two main aspects, as Juanita understood so clearly. Carmel's apostolate of prayer, sacrifice and intercession is for the world, and especially for priests. The individual Carmelite's striving for personal holiness and union with God is also apostolic and on behalf of the world and the Church. Carmel witnesses to the fact that this is true for all Christians, wherever they are and whatever their particular state of life. It is what Saint Paul meant when he described the Church as being a body, the Body of Christ, where, if one member suffers all the body is affected.[2] All Christians share in the holiness of Christ Himself, and by allowing that holiness to be active within them they are, as it were, channels of that holiness to the rest of the Church and to the whole human family.

Juanita said she loved other people so much that she thought it could weaken her love for God, although she recognized that her love for God actually increased her love for others and was at the same time an expression of her love for God. Separation from the world would not weaken that love if it were embraced with the right motives; indeed, if genuine, it increased that love. In Carmel her life would be one of unceasing prayer, keeping her in continuous contact with God; for her, this was the best way of manifesting her love for others:"Yes, in Carmel we begin to do what we'll be doing for all eternity: loving and singing the Lord's praises. And if this is what we'll be doing in heaven, isn't this the most perfect thing we could be doing now?"[3]

On her return to Santiago Juanita wrote to her confessor, Fr. Blanch, going into more detail about her doubts, and why she felt she needed an Order that devoted so much time to prayer, getting her to heaven more rapidly. For some time she had been aware that her life, like that of Saint Thérèse of Lisieux and Blessed Elizabeth of the

Trinity, was not to be a long one. What the Lord wanted to achieve in her had to be done swiftly. "What I want to know, Rev. Father, is where you think I'll become holy more quickly; for, as I've told you on different occasions, Our Lord has made me understand that I would not live a long life. Union with God is the essential thing. Where will I go to be united with God more quickly? I pray a lot that Our Lord will make known to me his divine will, because that's the only thing I'm looking for."[4]

Nevertheless she felt a strong attraction to the Sacred Heart Sisters. For one thing, she loved children, and was an excellent teacher. Sometimes when they were running catechism classes during their holidays, Rebecca would find herself without pupils because they had all gone to Juanita's class. It was understandable that she would have felt drawn to the Sacred Heart nuns, whom she had grown to love during her school years. An active order would give her a life of sacrifice in different ways from Carmel. In one sense, as Juanita recognized, she could find herself even more lonely as a Sacred Heart Sister than as a Carmelite Sister, because Sacred Heart sisters could be sent anywhere in the world, not even knowing the language, constantly having to adapt to new companions. The fact that they met with lay people meant that they had to be even more disciplined in their prayer life, to retain their religious spirit and the fruitfulness of their apostolate.

In trying to resolve her dilemma, Juanita put down the pros and cons of both Orders, listing their way of life and the differences between them. She also told Mother Angelica honestly of her doubts. The Sacred Heart apostolate was very attractive to her, and yet, she wrote, "the quiet and beloved convent, far from the noise of the world, whose gates open only to heaven, that life of prayer and union with God is strongly pressing me to go there. But suddenly, I think I should give up those attractions in order to win souls. It seems Our Lord is sending me all these doubts to test me, because when I'm at prayer, he makes me understand that I should become a Carmelite. But when prayer is over, the most terrible doubts spring up in this soul of mine, which felt it had obtained light from heaven and I slip back into deep darkness."[5]

It was a fruitful struggle, because it fixed in her the apostolic nature of Carmelite prayer. If she had gone to Carmel simply for her own holiness and an escape from the world, her life would have been sterile. But since she went to Carmel precisely to make herself holy, because that was the only way she could be fruitful for souls, then her life has had the impact and influence that it has.

Her dilemma could be resolved in only one way, and that was actually to make that long-awaited visit to the Carmel itself. Only her mother and Rebecca within the family knew of her intentions, so they had to wait for a suitable opportunity. This came on 7 January. The day before, her father suddenly decided to take the children along with him to the farm, even Miguel, who normally never went there. Her mother sent off a telegram to Los Andes, and the following day the two of them took the express train to Llay-Llay, where they were delayed for an hour before catching the Los Andes train. They had planned to reach Los Andes at 11:30, and then to return on the 2:10 train, but this delay, to Juanita"s delight, meant they could stay longer. They arrived at one o'clock, had lunch at a hotel, and reached the monastery at 1:45. Then Juanita had her first glimpse of the monastery in which she wanted to spend the rest of her life.

The monastery had been founded only 21 years before, in 1898, by Mother Margarite of Saint John of the Cross, who had been professed in the monastery of Saint Joseph in Santiago. The foundation first went to Viña del Mar, a seaside resort that was not very well populated and which did not have the resources to support them. They were therefore forced to transfer to Valparaiso in 1895, although they had to return to Viña del Mar in 1912, when a fire totally destroyed the monastery. The nuns attempted to make a foundation in Curimon when the people there begged them to come. Unfortunately, that town, too, proved to be too small to support them, and in 1902 they moved to Los Andes, a town nestling at the foot of the Andes and not far from the statue of the Christ of the Andes.

The monastery that Juanita saw was a very run-down and ugly old house that hardly looked like a monastery at all. In 1924, after Juanita's death, a larger Carmel was built, where the community lived until 18 October, when they moved ten miles away to Riconado Los Andes. This location was on part of the land that had once been part of her grandfather's hacienda, where Juanita had spent some of her holidays. The original Carmel where Juanita spent her religious life was badly damaged by an earthquake and was eventually destroyed. The land is now used by a fruit exporter.

Juanita immediately fell in love with the poor little Carmel. They were met by Sarita Urbistondo, the portress who looked after the extern, the outside part of the monastery. They were shown into the parlor where they met Teresita Montes, the sister of Chela Montes, Juanita's close friend, who had introduced her to the Los Andes community. Her mother stayed to talk to Teresita, while Juanita was shown into another parlor to meet Mother Angelica for the first time.

Mother Angelica had come with Mother Margarite from Curimon as Prioress of Los Andes, and she was also the Novice Mistress. She was born in Valparaiso in 1861, and had been the first postulant to be received in the newly founded monastery of Viña del Mar in 1889. She was a deeply spiritual and gifted person, and the bond between Juanita and Mother Angelica, forged by the correspondence they had had over the previous months, was confirmed by this meeting.

Mother Angelica described the Carmelite way of life to Juanita, its routine of prayer and work and the worship of God in the Divine Office, the Prayer of the Church. They broke off their talk to go into Vespers at 2:30, when Juanita was able to experience the Divine Office for herself. Mother Angelica gave her a Spanish translation of it so that she could follow the liturgy. It seemed to her as if she was in heaven in the dark little chapel, with the voices of the sisters behind the covered grille which separated the public chapel from the sisters' Choir. Juanita couldn't help tears of joy stream down her face at the thought that she would soon be joining them, and she saw Our Lord, his face smiling; it was, she said, the only time she saw him smiling, for in general she saw him with a sorrowing face.

At the end of Vespers, Juanita joined in the recitation of the Litany of Our Lady, the first prayer she shared with her future sisters. After Vespers, she returned to the parlor to meet Mother Angelica again and talked with her until 4:30. The Prioress confirmed that Juanita did have a Carmelite vocation, that she was indeed a born Carmelite. Her mother went off to have some tea—Juanita was too excited to want any herself—and then Teresita Montes came in to ask her if she wanted to make "the visit of visits," the presentation of an aspirant to the whole community.

Until now Juanita had spoken with Mother Angelica separated by grilles covered with a black curtain. This was now drawn back and the community came in with their veils raised. At that time there were 18 sisters in the community, including the two extern sisters. Juanita saw her sisters for the first time and was so overcome with emotion that she couldn't speak at first. The joy and the simplicity of the sisters soon put her at ease, however, and they were soon laughing and joking with each other. They sang an off-key song for her to make everyone laugh, then made Juanita stand up to see how tall she was—only two of the sisters were as tall as her. Juanita was totally won over by their joyful informality and the ease and sisterly love that was so evident among them. The novices confessed to her that they had been praying the Salve Regina every day for her, asking Our Lady that Juanita would soon join them.

There was no doubt in anyone's mind that this was the place to which the Lord was calling her, and the only question was when that day would be. Juanita said she wanted to enter in May, and one of the sisters ran off to find a calendar and see which feast day fell first that month, Saint Joseph or Pentecost. Saint Joseph won—his feast day then fell on the Wednesday of the second week of Easter, 7 May, and this was the day set for her entry into Carmel. She was also told the name by which she would be known in Carmel: Teresa of Jesus, after the great foundress of the reformed Carmel, Teresa of Avila.

The sisters then left, and Mother Angelica insisted that Juanita go and have some tea. She returned briefly afterwards for a final farewell, and to collect some books and other things she had asked for.

Juanita and her mother prayed that they wouldn't meet anyone they knew on the way home, and arrived back home at 11:30. Only Rebecca had stayed up to wait for them and to hear all their news; the rest of the family was totally unaware of what a momentous day it had been. As far as they knew, Juanita and her mother had simply gone out for the day to Llay-Llay.

Juanita had said farewell to the little monastery with the utmost reluctance, completely changed. She at last knew God's will for her without any doubts, and she was filled by the most overwhelming peace and happiness. She also knew that it was the Los Andes Carmel to which she was being called. In a letter to her first confessor, Fr. Colom, she revealed that she had been to the Carmel of Carmen Alto on the Alameda, but felt no attraction towards it. It did not have the poverty of Los Andes, it was less isolated, and she sensed a more "worldly" interest when talking to the Turn Sister, which was absent at Los Andes. Even the air of Los Andes was favorable, being much like that of Chacabuco, where her health had always been better.

In her letter to Fr. Colom, she listed the six considerations that drew her to Carmel: its prayer, solitude, poverty, penance and sacrifice, with its goal of praying for priests, as well as the sisters' purpose of sanctifying themselves for the holiness of the whole Church—and beyond.

Only four months now separated her from fulfilling an ambition that had pursued her during all her teenage years.

Notes

1. *Letter* 40
2. Cf. 1 Cor 12:12ff
3. *Letter* 40
4. *Letter* 45
5. *Letter* 46

Chapter 11
Preparing for Carmel

Juanita wrote to Mother Angelica the following day to express her joy and gratitude for their visit. By then she was busy with packing and seeing to the household as they prepared to travel, on 15 January, to a ranch in San Pablo their father had rented near Saint Javier de Loncomilla. Their father worked on the ranch, so they had the great joy of having him with them.

It was a long, nine-hour journey, and when they arrived they were keen to explore the neighborhood. Leaving some of the unpacking for later, they went for a walk along the Maule River with its spectacular view. They would have many outings among the picturesque scenery to enjoy the rustic surroundings and the quietness, which Juanita especially appreciated. As there weren't many families there, they didn't go horseback riding very much. With their sister Lucia now married, it was a smaller family group; and Juanita and Rebecca felt the strangeness of now being the elder daughters after being for so long the children of the family.

The only drawback was that there was no weekday Mass and sometimes no Mass on Sundays, and Juanita hungered for Holy Communion. She also found it difficult sometimes to have her times of prayer, as she had to join in with the family gatherings. Our Lord told her that she shouldn't allow her sadness and discouragement to show, but to keep serene and in control of herself. That would be her prayer and her surrender to his will. After all, she acknowledged that her whole life now was a constant prayer.

She continued to write to Mother Angelica, but had to be careful, for her father was the one who took any letters to the post box, and she was not yet ready to tell him her plans. With her entry into Carmel drawing ever closer, there were now practical things to discuss—what clothing she would have to have made up and buying the things she would need. She was now reading the Carmelite Constitutions and the Rule, and also Saint John of the Cross.

Despite her lack of solitude, her prayer was deepening. In prayer, Our Lord confirmed that she would be entering Carmel in May, and at the end of January, while she was praying before the Blessed Sacrament, she received further intimations of her future life:

> He told me then that He would like me to have a more intimate life with Him. He said I must suffer a lot, as well as other things that I don't remember. Since that time I've been much more recollected, and I saw Our Lord very clearly praying as if I'd seen a picture of Him. But I didn't see Him with my body's eyes, but just as He showed Himself to me. It was very vivid, and even though at times I wanted to represent Him in this way, I've been unable to do so. I saw Him that way, for more than eight days, but later I didn't see Him any more. And now I can't do it, either.
>
> Sometimes I've been very recollected in my prayer, and I was completely absorbed in contemplating God's infinite perfections, especially the perfection reflected in the mystery of the Incarnation. The other day something happened that I'd never experienced before. One night Our Lord made me understand His greatness and at the same time my nothingness. From that point on I wanted to die, to be reduced to nothing, in order not to offend Him nor be unfaithful to Him ....
>
> I've felt that love growing within me in such a way that I was thinking of God alone, even while

> doing other things. And I felt no strength within me,
> as if I'd fainted and were not in myself. I felt a strong
> impulse to pray and make a spiritual communion. But
> when I offered my thanksgiving, love overwhelmed
> me completely.[1]

At the same time she had an awareness of God's justice and the horror of sin. That is an understandable paradox: the closer one comes to God and understands his grandeur, the greater one understands the darkness of sin. It was a further spur to her to attain the holiness to which God was calling her.

A Mission then began, and the presence of the Heart of Mary missionary priests, who came over from Talca to run it, meant she was able to attend Mass and receive Communion. They had more than 500 Communions during the Mission, and once again Juanita was active in helping out with the catechism classes and the Masses. During the course of it, her mother gained fame as the "doctor lady": "The people here are lots of fun because they're not used to others running things, since almost all are property holders and people put on airs among them, so they were delighted when we dealt with them the way we did," Juanita wrote to Elisita. "They called my mother the doctor lady. You can't imagine the fame they brought her, because they came to her with a little boy, dying from a wound that covered his whole head. You could see down to the bone. We all thought he was going to die, because he was deathly ill. My mother gave him an injection, bandaged him up and in less than a month's time, he has fully regained his health."[2]

After the Mission ended Juanita and Rebecca went out on horseback or by buggy, visiting houses in the area to consecrate them to the Sacred Heart. They had over fifty children to teach, and since they discovered the children were being taught little or nothing of their faith in school, they continued the classes after the Mission finished. Once again, catechism was mixed with fun, and they organized a raffle, skits, and games for the children and showed them movies. All this was undergirded with intense prayer. Juanita spent an hour and a half in prayer each day before the Mission began; sometimes she felt as if she was fainting with love, unable to meditate in an active way but totally absorbed in the love of God. At other times she felt so unworthy of God that, in a purifying temptation, she considered the Lord should by right abandon her. The presence of Our Lord in the Blessed Sacrament so drew her that she would spend every moment she could there. Such intensity of love and sense of unworthiness meant she longed to undertake different mortifications: wearing a hair shirt, fasting, praying in uncomfortable positions, although only with her confessors' permission, and only when she could do it unobserved.

Her own prayer was deeply contemplative, fed by the simplicity of keeping herself in the presence of God throughout the day. She explained her own method in a delightful letter written to one of her friends:

> You tell me that you enjoy being God's little home. I'm very glad you feel that way, for in this, I see what you love. Sister Elizabeth of the Trinity used to say: "God is heaven and God is in my soul." We have heaven in our soul then. Well now, what do they do in heaven? They love, contemplate and glorify God. This is what we must do here: love Him above everyone else. One who loves is always thinking of the beloved. Let's think of Him continually, but, since that's impossible, at least let's think of Him very often. Let's contemplate Him there, in the depth of our soul, united to us. Let's contemplate Him praying to His eternal Father for souls and for sinners, and let's unite our-

selves with that divine prayer. Let's contemplate Him, working at our side. Now I look at Him as I write and unite myself with Him. Let's contemplate Him joyfully—says Saint Teresa—at Tabor, when we're happy; and sad, as he was in the garden, if we're sad; and do it that way in every situation. Let's contemplate Him in his creatures. Then it'll be easier for us to have charity. If we're humiliated, let's accept it for His sake. If we're praised, we're praised for Him. If we serve, we serve Him, and so on in all things. In this way the soul remains simple and united with Him; she is always thinking of and seeing Him. And finally, in heaven His praises are being sung and He's glorified in His works; let's be like Elizabeth of the Trinity then in praise of His glory.[3]

"And so Our Lord will be happy in our souls," she adds. Her prayer life enveloped all of her life and it was an ideal that others could imitate.

Juanita had hoped that Fr. Blanch would be coming, but this was not to be; instead, she received help from another one of the Mission priests, Fr. Julián Cea, with whom she would later keep up a correspondence. He had close contacts with the Carmelite Order, and before Juanita had disclosed her vocation to him, he kept teasing her that she had to have a Carmelite vocation. He had no hesitation in confirming her in her path of living in the continual presence of God in humility and purity, reflecting on the greatness of her God and her total dependence on him. They made a pact to pray for each other.

Late in February Mother Angelica sent her a package with examples of the clothing she would need in Carmel, so that she could make some up for herself. As Juanita still hadn't told her father of her plans she had to hide the package until she was sure she wouldn't be disturbed when she opened it; it touched her sense of humor to consider the lengths to which she and Rebecca went. She went into town with a jacket Mother Angelica had sent, hiding it underneath her jacket in order to smuggle it back into the house; then she and Rebecca took the coach out into the pine forest where they could try on the clothing without detection. Rebecca put on an apron under her dress while Juanita put on the waistcoat, giggling with the secrecy of it all. It eased somewhat Rebecca's unhappiness at the prospect of losing the sister whom she loved so dearly.

In a letter to Mother Angelica Juanita reported that both the garments were a bit too wide and short for her, and that she was also keen to have them made out of the poorest possible material. She was also concerned about the short postulant's cape, and whether she would be allowed to wear her Child of Mary medal on it; even after leaving school, she still continued to sign herself as "Child of Mary," so much did this mean to her.

Mother Angelica had obviously asked her for more details about her health, and Juanita gave her frank details. "I have no physical aliments, but I am very weak. I suffer fatigues quite frequently, and they begin in my stomach. Not really the stomach but rather the liver, and I spent all last year with a sharp pain in the chest and shoulders. I was examined by a number of doctors, and not one of them knew what I had. Finally Dr. Garcia Guerrero told me that it was the liver from where a nerve goes to my chest and shoulder, and that nerve was causing the pain. He gave me some medicine for my liver and I got better."[4]

The pain eased, but she was told always to wear a woolen skirt or other warm material to keep her stomach and liver warm. She was then anxious to be reassured that this illness would not affect her ability to become a Carmelite.

Juanita and Rebecca returned to Santiago on 7 March. Juanita spent two weeks at home, and then went on to her aunt and uncle's estate of San Enrique at Bucalemu for a week's holiday. Rebecca, unfortunately, wasn't able to go with her, because the nuns wouldn't allow her to take the time off school.

Juanita's health had much improved by this time, and her cousins so admired her stamina that they dubbed her "the Amazon." "I've gone horseback riding a lot," she wrote to her father, "and I'm fascinated with the ride up and down the hills, because it seems like I'm back in Chacabuco. I'm admired because I never get tired, and they tell me I have the stamina of an Amazon. There would be no end to my embarrassment, if that turned out to be so .... "⁵

They went trekking along the Rapel River, which flows through mountains covered with dense forests and among valleys and ravines. The area was totally mountainous, and they climbed up almost unscaleable cliffs, both on horseback and by car, along winding mountain roads, which would suddenly come out upon treacherous cliffs with sheer drops.

Juanita returned home 24 March and then had to face perhaps the hardest task of her life: to write to her father and ask his permission to enter Carmel.

"I'm going through real agony," she wrote to Fr. Cea. "I had hardly begun writing the letter, than I found again in myself the tremendous pain I feel at the thought of leaving my loved ones. What a struggle I fought against my own nature when I wrote the letter. And all the enthusiasm I'd been feeling for Carmel has gone away. It suddenly seems that what I'm about to do is really foolish; that it's all an illusion, etc. But now I see it's truly a wise thing and my will chooses it as a true good."⁶

In the long letter to her father she traced the path of her growing desire for Carmel. It was not a recent decision, she said, but one that had been growing over the years. She had at one time wanted to be happy, and wanted to know where she could find happiness. She desired to be very rich, but the experience of her own family demonstrated that wealth could very easily disappear. In thinking of love, she wanted a love that could never cool and never fail. So where could true happiness and wealth and love be found? "Then I understood that I hadn't been born for earthly things but for eternal ones. Why go on denying this fact any longer? Only in God has my heart found its rest. With God my soul found itself fully satisfied, so that I desire nothing in this world but to belong to Him completely."[7]

Writing the letter on the Feast of the Annunciation, 25 March, Juanita acknowledged that it was Our Lady who had planted the seed of her vocation within her, and it was Our Lady adding her pleading to Juanita's asking his consent. She also placed the matter under Saint Joseph's protection.

> Don't think, Daddy, that everything I'm telling you isn't breaking my heart to pieces. You know me well, and you know that I'm incapable of causing you any suffering on purpose. But even though my heart is bleeding, I must follow God's voice; it's necessary to leave the beings to which the soul finds itself intimately bound, in order to dwell with the God of love who knows how to reward the slightest sacrifice. How much more will He reward great sacrifices. Your daughter must leave these things behind. But keep in mind: that it is not for a man but for God. I wouldn't have done this for anyone else but for God who has an absolute right over us. Let that be your consolation: that I didn't leave for a man; and, that after God, it is you and my mother who are the ones I love most on this earth.[8]

Her father was still at San Javier in Loncomilla, and she posted the letter the following day so that he would receive it on the Saturday, Our Lady's day, to keep it all under her protection and prayers.

In the meantime, she wrote to her great friend Herminia at Cunaco. Santiago, she said, was empty of people; there were hardly any young people to go out with. She asked whether Herminia was preparing for her debut, and hinted that her own plans had already been laid for that year. She didn't want a debut for herself, of course, but wrote, "If they make us have a debut, let's do it willingly, that we can get to know some young men because at any rate, unless we become nuns we'll have to go along and deal with young men."[9] She admitted that she found the young men she knew to be very shallow, and none had pleased her. If they found no one to please them, then let them remain spinsters if they didn't become nuns, and do good without losing their freedom. This attitude, and her reluctance to go out to social events, worried and displeased her brothers, who at this point didn't know of her vocation. They kept urging her to go out more; and the day she sent the letter to her father, everyone, she wrote in her diary, was against her.

Juanita had an anxious wait for her father's reply, for he didn't answer immediately. After a few days he wrote instead to his wife; the letter arrived on 3 April, the day on which Lucia gave birth to their first little daughter, Luz, or Lucecita, as she was nicknamed. He believed he was obliged to give his consent, her father wrote, but needed more time to think it over. He would be coming home for the weekend to see his little granddaughter, and he would give his decision then.

Juanita found it hard to pray. She wanted to pray, but felt as if her soul was almost asleep, a thick cloud hiding Jesus from her. She tried to remain calm, at peace whatever her father's decision might be.

Don Miguel arrived home in the evening of 4 April, but even then didn't speak to Juanita straight away. Indeed, true to his inability to face up to difficult situations, he avoided being alone with her. He dearly loved his daughter, although Lucia was his favorite, and there are some poignant little remarks in Juanita's letters that showed how much she longed to receive more tangible tokens of his affection. "You can't imagine, Papa dear, how much I love you," she wrote. "But even before, when I was small, you didn't chat that much with us; now I understand you better and I've learned to appreciate your great heart."[10] The weeks she had been able to spend with him at San Javier meant a great deal to her, a precious memory she could take with her to Carmel, to make up for those many holidays the family had spent when he wasn't there with them. "I'll always remember the happy days I spent together with you," she wrote. "That memory will hold a special place in my heart that no one else can fill."[11]

Two days passed, with Juanita trying to speak to her father and he doing his best to avoid her. Then her cousins, the Valdès Ossa girls, contacted her and asked her to come with her father to their farm at Cunaco. Although her father decided not to go, Juanita said she would come, and she therefore had to have a decision before she left. She asked her father to come to her room and there he gave his consent. "If that's God's will," he told her, with tears in his eyes, "then I won't oppose it, since it will bring you happiness." It was Saint Joseph, she said, who had performed the miracle, since it was on a day dedicated to him. Her father agreed that the date should be 7 May. The road was clear now for Juanita to achieve her heart's desire, and she left that evening for Cunaco with a weight off her mind.

Notes

1. *Letter* 56
2. *Letter* 67
3. *Letter* 65
4. *Letter* 62
5. *Letter* 71
6. *Letter* 72
7. *Letter* 73

8. Ibid.
9. *Letter* 75
10. *Letter* 69
11. *Letter* 71

Chapter 12
Last Days at Home

As soon as she arrived at Cunaco, Juanita wrote to her father, thanking him for his consent to her entering Carmel. She had been unable to thank him properly at the time, because she was so overcome both by the pain of the approaching separation and by happiness at his consent. God would give all of them the strength they needed, she assured her father now, and "in the depths of your soul you'll experience the greatest satisfaction when you think that you've forever guaranteed your daughter's happiness."[1]

The week's break at Cunaco gave her a welcome change of scenery, with horseback rides with her cousins Chubby and Jaime, and day trips out in the car. Back home, in the meantime, there was the question of telling the rest of the family of Juanita's imminent entry into Carmel. This was solved inadvertently by her father, who accidentally left Juanita's letter to him lying around. Luis found it, read it, and furiously confronted his father. Don Miguel, to Juanita's gratitude, stoutly defended her, telling Luis that to oppose Juanita's vocation was like trying to stand in the path of an avalanche.

Although Juanita, his favorite sister, had not confided in him to save him suffering, Luis felt very bitter when he found out that both his mother and Rebecca had known of her intention for years. Even though on several occasions he had seen his sister totally absorbed in prayer, and reading the works of various Carmelite saints, the idea that she was contemplating Carmel for herself hadn't crossed his mind.

Her mother wrote to Juanita telling her that Luis now knew, and she immediately started a letter to him, but before she could post it received a letter from Luis himself. He couldn't understand, he wrote, that she, who was gifted with so many talents and abilities, should contemplate, as he saw it, squandering herself in an enclosed order. "You tell me that I should use the qualities God has given me for God's glory," Juanita replied. "Yes, it's true I have gifts, as you say, but how can I give greater glory to God than by giving myself over entirely to him and using my faculties, both intellectual and moral, day and night to know and love him? I have no beauty," she added, with a lack of self-awareness, "but if I were to have beauty, I wouldn't hesitate to offer it to him as well, because God deserves what's best and most beautiful."[2]

She assured him of her deep love for him: "Luis, you who are so loved, I'm speaking to you heart-to-heart. At this moment I'm feeling all the sorrow of our separation. I love you as I never loved you before. There are few brothers and sisters alive who are as close as the two of us."[3] He should know, then, that she sought happiness, a happiness that for her could only be found in Carmel. If she had been leaving home to get married and then discovered that Luis disapproved, she would have had no hesitation in breaking off the engagement. But her love for God could not be resisted:

> No, dear Luis, the love I have is above every created thing, and even though my own heart be trampled under foot, and torn to bits with pain, I won't fail to say my goodbyes, because I love him madly. If a man is capable of making a woman fall in love with him to the point that she leaves everything, do you not believe that God is capable of making his call irresistible to me? When one gets to know God; when in the silence of prayer he overshadows our soul with a ray of his infinite beauty; when he overshadows our mind with his wisdom and power; when he inflames us with his goodness and mercy; then everything on earth is seen with sadness ...."[4]

She realized that Luis wasn't able to understand all this now, but prayed that one day God's infinite goodness would reveal itself to him as it had revealed itself so overwhelmingly to her.

It had been arranged that her mother and Rebecca should come to Cunaco the following Sunday, and the three of them stayed until Wednesday before returning to Santiago, a couple of days later than intended. There were now only three weeks to go before her entry into Carmel, with many arrangements still to be made. Juanita followed the Holy Week liturgy, asking Fr. Cea to offer her up to God during the Good Friday liturgy, as she prayed for all her loved ones and the pain her decision was causing them. Her father, in the meantime, had returned to the farm, and Juanita wrote to him, sending him her prayers, as always, for a good harvest and the safety of his crops.

There were many letters to write, to friends and all the priests who had guided her over the years. At the beginning of April, Juanita had been to a Holy Hour led by a Jesuit priest, Fr. Antonio Falgueras, and had gone to confession to him. He was obviously interested in her spiritual progress and the special graces she received, and asked her to tell him of them. Juanita responded in a long letter that described the graces and experiences she had had since the age of seven. Twice, she said, she had seen vivid visions of Jesus. One night, "Our Lord revealed himself to me with such vividness that it seemed I could see him. He was crowned with thorns and his face was so sorrowful that I could not contain myself and began to cry so much that the Lord then had to console me in the intimate depths of my soul. This lasted for two minutes, more or less, and his face remained engraved for a long time in my memory."[5] This vision was the impetus that gave her a thirst for suffering and mortification that sometimes seems excessive, but which needs to be seen in the context of her calling to be a victim, sharing to a deeper degree in Our Lord's sacrifice on the Cross, and in the depth of her love for Jesus. "The love I had for Him kept growing stronger each day, and everything I suffered seemed very little to me," she wrote. "I mortified myself in every way I could. Once when the violence of love took hold of me, I grasped a needle and on my chest drew these letters: J.A.M., which means Jesus My Love. This did me harm, because it really exhausted me, but I never told anyone about it."[6]

Juanita had the discernment to distinguish visions that came from Our Lord and which she couldn't conjure up of her own accord, and visions that she felt came from her imagination, such as that of Our Lady: "Another time when I was praying some "Ave Marias" to make a crown for the Most Holy Virgin, everything disappeared from my sight and I saw over my Mother's head a crown filled with precious stones which gave off rays of light; but I didn't see her face. I think this was produced by my imagination, since it lasted but a second, and besides I'd been wanting to know if the Most Holy Virgin really accepted my prayers."[7]

Twice she received visions of Our Lord in the Blessed Sacrament, when he revealed Himself and His love to her in an almost sensible way while she was at school. "He made me understand His grandeur and told me then how He humbled Himself under the form of bread."[8]

The second vision had occurred the previous year, in which Our Lord revealed to her, her particular place in God's plan: "He told me He was praying incessantly to His Father for sinners, and that He offered Himself for them there on the altar. He told me that I should do the same, and He assured me that in the future He had chosen me with special preference over other souls, since He wanted me to live by suffering and consoling Him throughout my life. He said my life would be a true martyrdom, but that He would be by my side."[9]

His image remained within her for eight days with such vividness that she remained in constant prayer. When she tried to represent the vision to herself again after it faded she was unable to do so—an indication that this vision did not come from her imagination.

The locutions grew less as she grew older. Her present state of prayer was one of darkness in which she was unable to contemplate, despite her desire to do so, the "dark night" described by Saint John of the Cross, in which God's action was taking place at a deeper level than the soul can fathom.

Juanita wrote to her friend Elena, who was disappointed that she had chosen Carmel instead of the Sacred Heart Order, where Elena herself intended to enter. They wouldn't be living in the same convent, Juanita assured her, but they would be united in God and in their religious vocation. Lucia and Chiro, too, were told, and although they were upset, became resigned.

An aunt demanded confirmation from a priest she knew, who told Juanita that she should test her vocation further and delay her entry a further two months. This was a terrible blow, and her health began to suffer. Her mother felt that the priest, who seemed not to have much common sense and discernment, was speaking on the basis of what her aunt was telling him, rather than any true understanding of Juanita herself. Juanita therefore wrote to Fr. Falgueras, who told her to ignore what the priest said and carry on with her plans.

Other things added to her stress as 7 May drew near. There were so many friends and family to visit and to say her last farewells, which was tiring in itself without the emotional strain involved. Juanita had intended to burn her diary before she entered, but now both her mother and Rebecca were begging her for it, so they could keep it and read it as a constant reminder of her. She wrote to Fr. Blanch for his opinion, as she had lent it to him at one point. "What I want is to burn it in the fire, never to be seen by anyone," she wrote. "On the other hand, I can see that if people do read it, they will see the goodness of the Divine Master who has loved me so much, being that I am so ungrateful and a sinner."[10] Thankfully for the spiritual heritage of the Church, Fr. Blanch recommended that she hand the diary over to her mother and Rebecca.

Seven days before she entered, Juanita had some last photographs taken, one in secular clothes, which shows her serene beauty and poise, and another in the Carmelite habit. This was customary in Chilean Carmels at the time, when cameras were not allowed inside their convents.[11] One copy was given to her family, and the other was kept in the Monastery archives. The habit and white mantle were loaned by Sister Carmel of Saint Francis Xavier of the Carmel Alto monastery in Santiago.

One last bitter disappointment awaited her. Her father had intended to return to Santiago to be with her as she entered, but now he found he couldn't face it. "All I ask is that you come quickly before I go," Juanita pleaded with him. "It would be the greatest pain for me, if I were unable to hug you and kiss you for the last time. I assure you that the very idea that you won't come causes in me pain so intense that it becomes a physical weakness. My dear beautiful Daddy, please come. I can't resign myself to not giving you my last kiss and tender embrace. Remember that I love you madly. I can't believe that God wants me to undergo this horrible trial; but, anyway, may his adorable Will be done."[12] Her pleas fell on deaf ears, and she never saw her father again.

The day before she entered, Juanita went to the Church of National Thanksgiving, not far from their home, for a last prayer there. On her return home, she had a long talk with Luis, who was still unable to accept her decision. "You're taking away everything, and I don't even have God!" Luis told her. Juanita hugged him, leaned on his shoulder, and said to him, "Don't you experience God when you are with me?"

The day arrived at last, and her final act was to write to her beloved, wayward brother Miguel, leaving him her crucifix. Mindful of his self-destructive lifestyle, his heavy drinking and unsuitable friends, she assured him of her constant prayers:

> Believe me, my whole life will be a continual sacrifice of myself for you, that you may be a good Christian. Remember your Carmelite sister. When passions and friends want to immerse you in the abyss, your sister will always be at the foot of the holy altar begging strength for you. Remember that while you're giving yourself over to pleasures, she, behind the grilles of her cloister, will be subjecting her body to the harshest of penances. Yes, Miguel, I love you madly and, if it were necessary to lose my life that you might return to the right path and begin living a true Christian life, here is my life in God's hands."[13]

Despite being carefully prepared, the final meal at home was a strained experience. At one time the family had had ten servants and now there were only three, among them Juanita's dearly loved "mamita" and nurse Ofelia Miranda, and Rosa Mejía. Doña Lucia, who understood and supported Juanita's decision the most, tried to keep the atmosphere as normal as possible, but Rebecca and Luis were moody, and Miguel, who was normally talkative, had nothing to say.

Overnight, a huge electric storm broke, accompanied by heavy rains, which brought down many trees, and there was the possibility that trains might be delayed the following day. Rebecca was heartbroken and spent a sleepless night. Juanita was unable to fall asleep until the early hours of the morning.

Notes

1. *Letter* 78
2. *Letter* 81
3. Ibid.
4. Ibid.
5. *Letter* 87
6. Ibid.
7. Ibid.
8. Ibid.
9. Ibid.
10. *Letter* 90
11. The French Carmels had a different approach. Many photographs of Saint Thérèse of Lisieux and Blessed Elizabeth of the Trinity were taken.
12. *Letter* 91
13. *Letter* 93

Chapter 13
First Days in Carmel

Despite the storms the previous night, the trains were running after all. Before they set off, Juanita, as always, went to Mass with her mother.

Then, accompanied by her mother, Rebecca, Luis, Aunt Juana and a close friend, she took the express train to Los Andes, arriving at 11:30. However, they found that Juanita wasn't expected to arrive so early, so the party went to a nearby restaurant for a leisurely lunch, making those final moments together last as long as possible.

They then returned to the monastery and at long last the heavy wooden enclosure doors opened for Juanita, or Sister Teresa of Jesus, as she would henceforth be known. As she embraced Luis for the last time she whispered in his ear, "God exists, brother, and never forget that."

On the other side of the door the sisters, with their enclosure veils lowered, awaited her, and Sister Teresa knelt to kiss the crucifix that was offered her. For Rebecca the experience proved too much, and she fainted. Her relatives were in tears, but Teresa, true to her resolution to give all to God, was dry-eyed despite, as she wrote to her father afterwards, her heart being in tatters.

She was brought in procession to the Choir, with the sisters singing "O Gloriosa Virginem," and was left to pray for a while before the Blessed Sacrament. "She remained serene and tranquil," recalled her Prioress. "She had the look of an angel and a queen."

She then she went to the community room to be greeted by her new sisters. "I'm happy!" she said, filled with an unalterable peace, her radiant delight obvious to the community. She was no less delighted when she was taken to her cell and saw its poor simplicity. It contained a bed of wooden slats with a straw bed and hard pillow. Teresa had brought with her a mattress and pillow, much more comfortable than the Carmelite version, but was delighted when she was not obliged to use them. There was a jug and basin for washing, a low bench, a small workbasket and a low table before which she would sit on the floor to work. On the wall was a stark black wooden cross, hung with a crown of thorns but without a corpus, because it was for the Carmelite to put herself on the cross with her Lord. The cross bore the words of Saint Teresa of Avila: "God alone suffices," which became her motto.

A novice came along to her cell to become her "angel," the sister who would introduce her to the rules and customs of the house and guide her through the day with its routine of work, prayer and recreation. Her angel's first task was to help her on with the postulant's dress with its cape and veil. "I'm having a terrible time getting used to wearing sandals without backs," she wrote to her mother. "It makes me want to laugh when I see how awkward I am."[1]

Dressing herself the following morning, Teresa ended up with everything in disarray, disconcerted by the mere fifteen minutes allotted in which to dress and go down to Choir. "The second day I pulled a trick," she wrote to Rebecca, giving her newsy bits of information that she hoped her sister would enjoy. "I woke up at five, got dressed to the underskirt and laid down. When they sounded the bell, I put on the rest of my things and was the first to go out to sing the wake-up greeting which goes like this: "Praised be Our Lord Jesus Christ and the Virgin Mary, his Mother. Arise for prayer, Sisters, and praise the Lord." But after all that I couldn't sing the greeting because I didn't know where to do it."[2] Shortly, though, she would be assigned the task of rising early to wake the community herself, delighted that it gave her a precious time to be all by herself before the Blessed Sacrament before the sisters came into Choir.

Mealtime also had its difficulties, because she had to learn how to eat with a wooden spoon and a fork that were very small and narrow. It took her so long to eat that she was allowed to stay behind in Choir until the Community had eaten and then had her meal afterwards.

For the first few days she had no work to do, but wrote to her family, who in their turn lost no time in writing to her, even eight year old Ignatio. The Sisters, ever mindful of the sacrifice their families had made when they themselves had entered, made sure that new entrants kept in touch with their families, to ease the separation.

The community also had some dogs. One of them, a big, silver-colored dog called Molzuc, became her firm friend. Mother Angelica introduced Teresa to the dog with a gift of bread to sweeten the meeting, because he could be quite fierce with strangers. However, Molzuc took to Teresa straight away; "Look. Even the dogs love her!" one of the sisters remarked.

Eight days, and it felt as if she had always been in Carmel. "I'm happy, dear little sister," she wrote to Elisa, who also wanted to enter Carmel. "I'm the happiest creature in the world. I'm beginning my life in heaven, of adoration, praise and unending love. It seems to me as if I'm already in eternity, because you don't feel time here at Carmel. We're immersed in the bosom of the Unchanging God."[3]

The Carmelite day gradually took shape for her. The Sisters rose at 5:15; at 6 o'clock they had an hour of prayer, then the Hours of the Divine Office were said. Mass followed, and then at 9 o'clock the novices went to the Novitiate for instruction and for permissions for the day. Mother Angelica, as well as being Prioress, was also Novice Mistress. Afterward they had breakfast in the Novitiate oratory, putting their cups on low benches and sitting on the floor. They then went to tidy their cells, and Sister Teresa swept the Novitiate corridor, then went to her cell until 11:00 to sew. They made their own altar linen and their own clothes. Teresa was very impressed that the sisters' habits were so darned and patched that often there was none of the original material left. The main meal of the day was preceded by a five-minute examination of conscience.

Teresa assured Rebecca that she was never hungry, and described the sort of meal they had: the novices had a soup made of meat—the Carmelite Rule forbade meat except for the sick and infirm, and this was a way of breaking the young postulants in gently to the Rule. They would have a dish of green beans "like Uncle Pancho used to make," she added.[4] This was followed by fruit, and tea made with milk. The sisters took turns doing the washing up; Teresa said that the first time she did it she forgot to put the covers on the washbasins and water began spilling out. One of the extern sisters came to her rescue and prevented a flood.

The community then had recreation together until about 1:15, followed by devotions and free time until 2 o'clock. Vespers was said at 2 o'clock, with spiritual reading from 2:30 until 3 o'clock. There was work until prayer, which was from 5 until 6, followed by supper, with an hour's recreation afterwards. Compline was said after recreation, with Matins at 9 o'clock. Everyone was in bed by 11 o'clock.

A week after she entered, Sister Teresa had to read the lessons at Morning Prayer in Latin. It was a daunting experience, but afterwards the Sub-Prioress, who is in charge of the Choir, came to the Novitiate with a tray of fruits, chocolates, brown sugar sweets and biscuits, a custom in that Carmel when a young sister did her first reading. The Divine Office, the Prayer of the Church, soon became a revelation and a delight to her. "She formerly had only a vague idea of it," wrote Mother Angelica. "At Carmel she penetrated its grandeur, and her spirit felt itself transported with devotion and joy when reciting the psalms inspired by God himself. She could now render him worship through the appropriate ceremonies. She united herself to the angels in order to offer this worship of adoration and love. She appeared to be one of them, leaving the earth in order to unite herself with the blessed ones of heaven in the worship which they render to His Divine Majesty."[5]

Teresa made few notes of her inner life while in Carmel, but on 14 May she did write some notes that give an indication of the total gift of herself that she was making:

> I'm now in Carmel 8 days. Eight days of heaven. I feel divine love in such a way that there are moments when I believe I'm unable to endure it. I want to be a pure host and continually sacrifice myself for priests and sinners. I made my sacrifice without tears. What strength God gave me in those moments. How I felt my heart torn to pieces on hearing the sighs of my mother and brothers. But I held on to God and He alone was enough. Our Lord reproaches me for my minor imperfections and asks the smallest sacrifices, but it's inconceivable how much they cost me. He asked me to live in continual recollection and to look at no one. And I'm to do everything out of love. I should obey at the slightest indication and have a great spirit of faith. [6]

Three days later she described an experience in prayer she had that further increased her understanding of her sacrificial role.

> I am greatly aware of divine love. In prayer I felt that the Sacred Heart was united to mine. And His love was so great that I felt my whole body embraced in that love and yet with no experience of my own body. All this touched me so that I had to sit down and a sensation so disagreeable was produced in me that I began to quiver. The love of God was so manifested to me in

such a way that I was unaware of what was happening.
I spent almost an hour and three-quarters in this way.
Our Lord told me that I should abandon myself totally
to Him and that I would attract many souls to abandon
themselves completely. I offered myself as a victim
so that He would manifest His infinite love to souls.
He told me that I should do all this by uniting myself
to Him.[7]

A few days after that she went to the community's confessor,
Father Avertano of the Most Blessed Sacrament, who was also a Carmelite, and gave him a full account of her prayer, and especially the
locutions she received. He advised her not to pay any attention to any
voice she should hear interiorly if it commanded her to do something
extraordinary, and that if the command was repeated four times she
should then consult him. Teresa had written of "abandonment," and
this was something Fr. Avertano also stressed. Her one aim should be
God's will. She shouldn't seek or ask for the cross, but accept what
trials were given her. She should not to draw attention to herself, either
to seek affection or to be despised, and should be equally at ease with
all her sisters. Mother Angelica was aware that she would be over-
enthusiastic in seeking mortifications and penances, and Fr. Avertano
also warned her against excessive practices. One should not to seek to
kill the body, but to inconvenience it. It was unsought trials that would
hurt the most, and that evening Teresa was almost overwhelmed with
homesickness and the pain of separation from her family.

She wrote:

At night I felt an immense pain of separation. I was
imagining Rebecca alone in our room and crying. I ar-
dently desired to hug and embrace each of the ones I left
for Jesus. I didn't know the pain I was going through
and whether I should tell this to our dear Mother Su-

perior, since it seemed to me that I was seeking consolation from creatures. But I told Our Lord that if she
comes in to leave us in the novitiate, I'll tell her; oth-
erwise, I'll be silent. But Our Lord, as usual, spoiled
me and, contrary to custom, permitted her to come. I
told her my sorrow and she took me to the choir where
I began to tremble because of the violence of the pain.
Thanks to the prayers of our dear Mother I remained
more in peace and was able to sleep afterward.[8]

The effect on her family of her entry in Carmel indeed gave her immense pain. Rebecca was so distressed that she suffered a breakdown.
She sometimes fell down in a faint if anything happened in connection
with her sister. In her letters to her, Teresa would try to assure Rebecca
that even if physical distance and circumstances separated them, in
Jesus they were united. Why do you feel so alone?" she wrote. "Aren't
we always really one in our Divine Master? Can you be thinking that
your Carmelite sister has no room in her heart to love the one who is
part of her very being ... ? You are with me always; we are still working together. Don't be afraid of my forgetting you. I've loved you too
much to forget you so easily. I love you more than before, because love
is not merely words but deeds. Now I work, now I sacrifice myself
for you that you may know God's will."[9] She was very concerned that
Rebecca wanted to leave school, and urged her strongly against it.

Luis, too, suffered greatly at losing his beloved sister, whom he
described as "the angel of our home, the treasure of our household,"
and was so embittered that what faith he had remaining from his philosophical doubts was destroyed. The most he could promise Teresa was
that he would be good for her sake. "This I cannot allow," she replied.
"Let's never do good for a miserable creature. Love and do good in
order to possess unchanging Goodness eternally, the infinite Good, the
only One who can fill and satisfy your will."[10] She knew it was useless

to argue against his doubts; all she could do was to direct him to listen
to the God who dwelt within him and who loved him so completely:
"Luis, pray! Reflect calmly on who God is and on who you are and
on all that you owe him. After classes, go by the church where Jesus
is alone, and he will speak to your heart in mystical silence. Join me
in spirit. At five o'clock I'm praying. Let's accompany the God who
is abandoned, and let's ask him to give us his holy love."[11]

Miguel was still causing his mother immense problems, and she
went so far as to say the Lord ought to take him before he slipped further into his dissolute lifestyle. Teresa pointed to the Good Shepherd
who would leave the ninety nine to go after the one that had strayed,
and said that she herself needed to give herself even more to God for
her brother's sake.

In all her letters she drew people to the presence of Jesus in the
Blessed Sacrament. In the two visions she had had of Our Lord in the
Blessed Sacrament, he had called her to offer herself, as he offered
himself on the altar, in unceasing prayer and intercession for sinners.
This was where her heart was, and where she saw the pattern of her
own self-giving, in her own words, "to be a host."[12]

Teresa was shortly given her assigned tasks. Besides the sewing,
which all the sisters did, she was assigned to help in the garden and
was soon writing to her family to ask for carnations, roses, fertilizer
and garden vegetables. She also asked to work in the kitchen to learn
how to cook.

On Sundays the sisters entertained themselves with singing, accompanied on the guitar and bandurias, and Teresa was soon writing to her
family asking for favorite pieces of music for them to learn, as they didn't
have a wide repertory. She wrote, too, to ask Rebecca for the materials
she needed to make little woven baskets, holy cards, and plaster to make
medallions. It would be Mother Angelica's Feast Day on 13 June, and it

was the custom for the sisters to make little gifts for her, which would then be distributed to friends, families and visitors to the Carmel.

After less than a month in Carmel it felt like home, and as if she had never been anywhere else.

Notes

1. *Letter* 95
2. *Letter* 98
3. *Letter* 101
4. *Letter* 108
5. *Testimonies*, p. 45
6. *Diary* 54
7. Ibid.
8. Ibid.
9. *Letter* 103
10. *Letter* 107
11. Ibid.
12. *Diary* 56

Chapter 14
Cenacle Retreat

Before they celebrated the Prioress's Feast Day, the sisters had their Cenacle retreat, the ten-day period between the Ascension and Pentecost when the disciples had gathered for prayer around Mary in the Upper Room, awaiting the gift of the Holy Spirit. Juanita wrote to her mothr, "How happy I found myself, alone with the One who alone lives!" She continued:

> Mummy, I wish you could read my soul and see all that Our Lord has written in it during these days. I wish you could see my soul filled with the radiance of the Divine Prisoner. With what is written there, with that fire, he makes me understand and lets me see things unknown, a grandeur never before seen. You can't imagine, Mummy, the change I see in myself. He has transformed me. He keeps drawing back the curtains that hid him, which, there in the world, amidst the darkness, one cannot perceive. He seems more and more beautiful to me, more tender, more passionate.... May I have no other attraction than to know him that I may love him, love him madly.[1]

In her diary she described in more detail what was happening in her:

> Our Lord told me I should go to the Father through Him. The one thing I should strive for in this retreat is to hide and submerge myself in the Divinity in order to know God better and to love Him, and to know myself better and to abhor myself. He desires me to allow myself to be guided entirely by the Holy Spirit. My life should be a continuous praise of love. I should lose

myself in God and always contemplate Him without
ever losing sight of Him. For this reason, I should live
in silence and forgetfulness of all created things, since
God by His nature always lives alone. In him, all is
silence, harmony, unity. And to live in Him it's necessary to become simple, to have no other thoughts or
activity: to praise.[2]

The influence of Elizabeth of the Trinity is very strong in these
notes: her emphasis on silence, simplicity and praise, the trinitarian
form of prayer to the Father, through the Son, in the Holy Spirit. But
Teresa puts her own distinctive stamp on it; her praise was to be a
praise of love.

She called herself a trinitarian. "Every day I reverence, admire and
love the Holy Trinity more," she wrote to Elisa Ossa. "I've found at
last the centre, the place of my rest and recollection, and I want you,
little echo of my soul, to find Him there, too. Let's live within the Heart
of Jesus contemplating the great mystery of the Holy Trinity, that all
our praises and adoration may come forth made perfect by the Heart
of our Jesus, and united with His own. Let's live in unity with Our
Lord's Humanity and be plunged into His Divinity.[3] It was through
Our Lord's humanity, and especially through the humanity expressed
in his Sacred Heart burning with love for us, that she entered into the
very life of the Trinity.

From reading Thérèse of Lisieux she came to a deeper understanding of her vocation to be a victim of love. With Thérèse she had a thirst
for souls. "What I feel is insatiable hunger and thirst that souls may
turn to God and seek Him not out of fear but with unbounded trust
in His Divine Love."[4] These sentiments are pure Thérèse. But when
she drew on the spirituality of her fellow Carmelites, it was never a
slavish copying. It was a true expression of her life. She added an

extra dimension of her own, which was joy in the presence of God. Her joy in God was so intense that she longed for others to share in that joy, too. She had a deep sense of the presence of God always with her, even in darkness; that was her joy and happiness, and she could express it in delightful ways. "Since today is Sunday, we don't have many chores," she wrote to her mother, "so Rev Mother is letting me travel your way for a few minutes chat with you. But now I'll have to put two chairs out, because Jesus is coming, too. It's impossible to separate us now. What happiness...."[5]

Her prayer during the retreat was indeed the sleep of the senses described by Saint John of the Cross:

> God is communicating himself to my soul in so inef-
> fable a way during these days in the Cenacle. The love
> I feel is not sensible, but much more interior. In prayer
> there are things happening that never happened be-
> fore: I remain completely steeped in God. I can't make
> reflective prayer. It's as though I'm sleeping in God. In
> this way I experience His greatness and so great is the
> joy I'm experiencing in my soul, as something coming
> from God. It seems to me that I find I'm completely
> immersed by the divinity.[6]

Reading Saint John of the Cross made her realize that it was God who was leading her from meditative prayer to a different, more contemplative form of prayer. Writing to her friend Elisa shortly afterwards, she suggested that Elisa, too, was being drawn to the same form of prayer, and advised her to buy a copy and read Saint John of the Cross:

> Believe me, on several occasions it brought me lots
> of comfort. Don't be discouraged if you can't make
> discursive prayer or don't know what to say to Our
> Lord. He's well aware of how miserable we are. Who

would know what to say to the Word, the eternal Word, the divine and uncreated Wisdom? The same thing has happened to me many times and I don't think my prayer is bad because of it, because the goal of prayer is to kindle in us the love of our God. When we're there in His presence, if just gazing on Him is enough to make us love Him, and if we are so captivated by His Beauty that we can't say anything but that we love Him, why, little sister, should we be upset?[7]

During the retreat she had an experience in prayer that could have been noticed by others in the community, and which, if it had been noticed, would have given her great embarrassment, since she never wanted to appear different from everyone else. Only one or two other sisters knew of the exceptional graces given to her, apart from Mother Angelica:

Three or four days ago while I was in prayer, I felt God was abasing Himself to me, but with such great impetus of love that I believe that if it had lasted just a little more I'd have been unable to endure it, because in that moment my soul was about to leave the body. My heart was beating with such violence that it was awful. I felt that my whole being was as though suspended and that it was united with God. They rang the bell and I didn't hear it. I saw other novices leave and tried to follow them but was unable to move. It was as though I were nailed to the ground. Almost to the point of tears I begged Our Lord to allow me to leave since all were going to notice this. Then I was able to get up, but my soul was as if in another place.[8]

This was not the only grace that was given her. On the Feast of Pentecost she had another experience in prayer, when she felt her "whole being carried off in God with great violence, without being able to conceal it. Three times I returned to myself and was then again transported. I suffer greatly, since I don't know if these are illusions, and I don't have anyone to consult about this matter. Finally, I surrender myself to God's will. He's my Father, my Spouse, my Sanctifier. He loves me and desires my well-being."[9]

In contrast with these experiences were times when she had horrible doubts against faith, that even went so far as to doubt the presence of the Lord in the Blessed Sacrament. Mother Angelica considered that she humiliated herself too excessively and that she "should be more of a woman." This self-humbling was due to the light Our Lord was giving her in her own sinfulness and the perfection to which he was calling her. The periods of doubt increased her humility, and also her capacity to receive even more of God.

Teresa was tempted to believe that all these experiences in prayer were illusions, and also that the sisters were noticing that there was something strange in her. Indeed, one of the sisters did not take to her at all.

When the retreat ended, Teresa wrote to Luis, longing to share with him the love that flooded her soul:

> How I'd like to share with you what I feel, little brother of my soul. How I'd love to show you the lovely, infinite, horizon beyond creation that I experience and contemplate. I love God now a thousand times more than I did before, because I hadn't known Him. He reveals and makes Himself known to souls that really seek to know and love Him. Everything on earth, Luis, seems to shrink, to lose value before the Divinity which, like an infinite Sun, continues to shine upon my miserable soul with its rays. Oh, if you could go to the depths of my soul even for an instant, you'd see me captivated by that Beauty, by that incompre-

hensible Goodness. How I'd love to bind the hearts of
creatures and surrender them to divine Love! You've
never known the heaven that I, through God's mercy,
possess in my heart. Yes. I have heaven in my soul,
because God is there, and God is heaven.[10]

The inability of Luis to believe as she believed, the seeming im-
possibility of her experience being passed on to others, caused Teresa
great pain. But there is timing in God's grace; each person is totally
individual, and God's action in souls is individually tailored to their
needs and their ability to respond. Nevertheless, the graces given to
one person within the Body of Christ are never for that person alone, as
Teresa was profoundly aware. As we have seen, this interdependency
of Christians within the Body of Christ is a truth that is at the heart
of the contemplative vocation. As well as being an example and an
inspiration for others to follow, a soul totally open to the grace and
action of God, as Teresa was, is a gift to the whole Body of Christ, and
enriches everyone, not only within the Church but also throughout the
whole human family.

In the future, it was Luis, with his trained legal mind and analyti-
cal abilities, who put this principle into concise words, showing how
well he was eventually able to understand what motivated Teresa in
Carmel: "A Carmelite is certainly a missionary who never goes out,
never leaves her cell. Perhaps the Carmelite never sees or hears the
ones she saves, but she knows how many she saves although they are
far away. Just as in the conservation of energy in the physical world,
nothing is destroyed or lost in the world of souls. According to faith
in Christ, the merit of one is in solidarity with the sinfulness of the
other. Everything circulates, compensates for all else and is shared,
although invisibly, through God's loving action."[11]

Perhaps it was in the grace of God's plan that Teresa's vibrant and luminous faith needed to be confronted by Luis's philosophical doubts, doubts that would be one of the dominant traits of the twentieth century with the rise of atheism and agnosticism in the Western world. She could confront those doubts not only with her well reasoned, educated and lucidly argued understanding of her Christian faith, but also, and even more, with the evident action of God's love living and shining out from her, a love so irresistibly attractive to all with whom she came in contact. She demonstrated in her own self that faith and love could take on doubt and unbelief and not be defeated.

The Retreat ended with the Feast of Pentecost, and the community had a few days of holiday when the normal rules were relaxed. June 13 was the Prioress's Feast Day when the sisters gave her the small gifts they had made. Teresa was delighted with the joy and informality of the occasion. "Believe me I've been really touched by the simplicity and love here among the sisters," she wrote to Rebecca. "There are no ceremonies or speeches, and everyone crowds around Rev. Mother to look at her gifts. Every day I thank God more for finding myself in this delightful little dovecote, among so many saints. You can't imagine how holy these sisters are. I hold them in veneration and grieve to see myself so naughty and unworthy. They have to pray a lot for me that I may become a holy Carmelite and pray quickly, too, right?"[12]

The month of June is the month devoted to the Sacred Heart, a devotion that Teresa loved. Although she had not, after all, entered the Sacred Heart Order, she kept her deep devotion to the Sacred Heart. In a letter to her friend Carmen, she described how she entered into this devotion, and invited Carmen to "enter into His Divine Heart, where I live submerged, breathing only on the divine, and consuming my many miseries in the fire of His love. That's where I live, contemplating the grandeur of His Divinity. First I look at God—that incomparable Trinity—plunging myself into the bosom of my Father, of my Spouse, of my Sanctifier; and then I look at the eternal Word made flesh, at my Divine Jesus. That's when I sing my praise of glory and of love.[13]

. Fr. Falgueras had told her to contemplate God, and above all Jesus Christ, since his humanity is the gate through which we must pass to enter into the Divinity. Pondering on entering into the sentiments and affections of the Sacred Heart led her to imitation of Jesus and transformation into his life.

She had time to write a letter to her friend, Elisa Ossa, on 13 June; the letter was a long meditation on the Sacred Heart. She linked it with the presence of Christ in the Eucharist as well as with his passion; understandably, because they are all reflections of the person of Christ and the revealing of his life to us. The pictorial representation of the Sacred Heart as revealed to Saint Margaret Mary shows the Heart of Jesus surrounded by a crown of thorns, since he revealed his love for us most profoundly and totally in suffering and dying for us on the cross. The devotion to the Sacred Heart itself arose from the contemplation of the pierced side and heart of Jesus as he died on the cross. He extends that love for us by remaining with us continually in the tabernacle, a prisoner of love. Teresa said she sometimes longed to be freed of this life in order to be totally free to love God untrammeled with the limitations of life on earth. But then, seeing how Jesus circumscribes himself within the host and within the tabernacle, she realized that this was the way Jesus wanted her to follow for the present: hidden, silent, self-giving.

Love calls out to love, and Teresa was profoundly conscious of how poor her love was in response to the love of Jesus that so overwhelmed her. The representation of the Sacred Heart that is so familiar and so representative of the Catholic faith takes us to the heart of the Gospel.

It reminds us that Jesus is saying to us that what we see is what he is: Love. Teresa lived in that love:

> He sees that I want to love Him but that I still don't have enough strength in my soul to possess the love as strong as death. Our Jesus is all Heart. And now He has captured mine. He keeps me imprisoned in the furnace of His love. I live in Him, sister dear. What peace, what sweetness, what silence, what an ocean of beauty encircles that Divine Heart! How He fills me with His tenderness, despite my being so unfaithful to Him. When will that happy day dawn when death, having broken the chains of sin amid which we live, we can finally tell our God: "We will never again offend you, and no one, nothing can separate us from you."[14]

Notes

1. *Letter* 106
2. *Letter* 109
3. Ibid.
4. *Letter* 104
5. Ibid.
6. *Diary* 56
7. *Letter* 109
8. *Diary* 56
9. Ibid.
10. *Letter* 107
11. *Testimonies*, p. 91
12. *Letter* 108
13. *Letter* 105
14. *Letter* 109

Chapter 15
Clothing Day

The period of postulancy, the first stage of the religious life, normally lasted six months, but Teresa wrote to Fr. Colom on 20 July that Mother Angelica had already approached the Nuncio to dispense Sister Teresa from this ruling so that she could receive the habit on 15 October, the Feast of Saint Teresa of Avila, her patroness. Teresa said she had a burning desire to receive the habit, yet on the other hand she felt acutely that she still fell far short of the holiness to which she was called.

She was still experiencing the agony and ecstasy of the various trials she went through during the Pentecost retreat. On the one hand, her prayer was growing more and more simple. "I hardly begin to pray when I feel my entire soul immersed in God, and I find a peace and such great tranquility that I can't describe it," she wrote to Fr. Colom. "Then my soul perceives that divine silence, and the more profound the quietude and recollection becomes, the more God reveals himself to me. It is a very clear and sudden thing. It's not by reflecting. Rather I get upset when I reflect. When this knowledge becomes very clear, I feel as though my soul wants to flee away from my being. I'm unable to feel my body."[1]

Sometimes she felt as if she couldn't move, and when a sister came up to speak to her she heard the words as if from a distance. She felt as if she was inflamed with God's love, as though he were communicating his own fire to her.

She was continually afraid that her experiences were an illusion and made sure she asked advice on them. One priest whom she consulted told her to reject the thought of God, but this caused her immense distress. Fr. Avertano, on the other hand, told her not to resist but to follow what God was doing in her.

At other times she felt weighed down by the sense of her unworthiness and sinfulness, as if God had abandoned her, and she experienced temptations against faith. She felt as if left in total darkness, doubting even God's existence. On 18 July these feelings were so strong that she thought she was in a state of mortal sin and refused to go to Holy Communion. Mother Angelica said that she should ignore the temptation, but overnight decided that if her conviction was so strong she should not oblige Teresa to receive Communion against her will. It was a humbling experience for her, even though it lasted but a day. It left her very humble not only in the presence of God but also in the sisters' presence, who couldn't fail to notice that she hadn't gone to Communion and that she went to Confession afterward.

Looking back, she could discern that even these dark experiences had drawn her closer to God, with him communicating himself even more profoundly after the dark times had passed.

While being in Carmel herself, Teresa was influencing her friends, either to serve God in the world, or attracting them to the religious life. Her cousin Elisa was still struggling with her longing for Carmel, but it was becoming clearer that she would not be able to enter. Because of her love for Elizabeth of the Trinity, Teresa called her Isabel, the Spanish for Elizabeth, and pointed her to Elizabeth's example. She reminded her that when Elizabeth thought that she, too, might not be able to enter Carmel she tried to be a "Carmelite in the world." Teresa thought, rightly, that Elisa would not enter Carmel, and for the time at least, she should remain with her family. "In the meantime you can be a Carmelite in the world. God wants you to be. He'll give you the strength and grace you need to be a Carmelite. May Jesus, in that desert of love, find a place of refreshment in His Isabel. May He find,

amidst the darkness of the world, a fire of love in your pure heart....
Our Lord spent 30 years of His life in retirement and prayer, and only
dedicated but three years to evangelizing. In the Most Holy Sacrament,
he continues that uninterrupted prayer. In heaven the occupation of our
souls will be to adore and to love. Let us begin, then, on earth what
we'll be doing for all eternity!"[2]

Her friend Chubby was also trying to live a prayerful life in the
world, and amused Teresa with her efforts to avoid unwelcome attention: "As for all you tell me about your walks on the Alameda, all I
could do was laugh, for I see you with your goal of fishing passing
through the young men in a virginal way, with your eyes cast down in
a virginal way, with your hat half way down on your head, walking at
a rapid pace with a postulant's hairstyle. Isn't that the way it was?"[3]

She was pleased that Rebecca was experiencing a greater love of
God, even though separation from her beloved sister was still causing her great grief, and even hoped that Rebecca, too, might have a
religious vocation. "How greatly I pray for you, my dear little Dove,
that you may belong completely to Jesus! Now there's no difference
between us. The little house of our souls has but one Master, the same
Sun shining upon them, and this Master is our Jesus."[4]

In the meantime, she had a more mundane task for her sister. One
of the monastery dogs was partial to chewing up an occasional letter
or two, but then had got into her cell and chewed up a little notebook
Mother Angelica had lent her, containing thoughts of Father Avertano.
Now she had to return it. Could Rebecca write it all out for her in a
similar notebook, in her best handwriting?

On the Feast of Saint Martha at the end of July, the sisters in the
Novitiate took over from the lay sisters who worked in the kitchen,
cooking all the meals for the community and giving the lay sisters a
welcome holiday; it was an enjoyable holiday in Carmel for everyone.

She wrote, "You can't imagine how much we enjoyed ourselves preparing the meals. We laughed at the top of our voices, when we saw
ourselves weeping as we peeled the onions. Everything in Carmel is
done with joy, because wherever we are we have Jesus with us, who
is our infinite joy."[5]

A few days later, she was delighted to be given charge of the sacristy. Given her deep love and reverence for the Mass and the Blessed
Sacrament, it meant so much to her to be close to the vessels that
would be used on the altar, and to the hosts that would be consecrated
to become the Body of Christ.

The Mass was the center of her life. Holy Communion was the
food she needed to draw her into ever closer union with Our Lord, and
she never ceased to encourage her friends and family to go to Mass
and receive Holy Communion frequently, if they wanted to deepen
their own spiritual life.

She had also meditated deeply on the presence and the self-giving of Our Lord in the tabernacle, seeing there examples for herself
in her Carmelite life. She developed these thoughts in her long letter
to Elisa:

> Eli, a Carmelite is a host, as I told you. Jesus is a Host
> on the altar. He hides Himself. A host, apparently, does
> not see or hear, or speak, or complain. Isn't that true?
> In the same way, if we ourselves want to be hosts, we
> must hide from the gaze of others. Let's hide ourselves
> in God, that is, let's work always never to seek ap-
> proval or receive sympathy and love from others but
> always have God as the witness and purpose of our
> actions. A host, Eli, has no will of her own. To obey
> without answering back and to obey even what seems
> contrary to our own judgment, to be silent for God. To
> obey Him. To obey without showing that it costs us, or
> that which is commanded is displeasing to us.

The Sacred Host is in a little ciborium. We, as hosts, should seek poverty, choosing the least appealing things for ourselves, without others noticing it. We must seek what is less comfortable for ourselves in all things and everywhere.

The Sacred Host is pure. We should flee from the affection of every creature. Our heart is for Him alone, Eli, it belongs only to Him. We should flee attachments to things vain, subdue our passions and when our body craves what is comforting or what spoils us, do just the opposite.

The Sacred Host is given to human beings. We should give ourselves over entirely, or better still, offer ourselves—for it's not suitable to be given—to everyone around us. This will make us charitable, but always seeing Jesus in our neighbor. Let's resolve to do this, Isabel dear, my Carmelite sister; let's make this challenge to see who arrives at the goal first.[6]

As well as the sacristy, Teresa was also given the Novitiate and its oratory to look after and keep tidy, which, although it was small, took her a long time. She had never been used to doing housework or gardening, so everything was a learning process for her, and she wasn't able to do such tasks quickly. "Often perhaps when I'm sweeping or straightening up my little cell, I think that in my life I might not have needed to do this," she wrote to Mama Ofelia and Rose Mejias, two dearly loved family servants. "Yet, for Jesus, I've preferred to be poor and to work. Since he became poor for love of me, I want to do the same for love of him. When I think that, I feel happy, even though I'm tired."[7]

In the middle of August she had a retreat day, alone with the Alone, spending almost all day in Choir. The previous day, the Feast of the

Assumption, she had also spent six hours in Choir, in addition to the Divine Office.

There was another community celebration at the end of August when Sister Mary of Saint Joseph, the Infirmarian, celebrated her silver jubilee. Teresa wrote to her mother asking her to buy half a dozen spoons and a small statue of the Holy Family that she could give to Sister Mary of Saint Joseph as gifts: Sister Mary's own statue of the Holy Family was completely worn away.

Teresa also received visits from Mama Ofelia and her governess, and other family friends. Rebecca also wanted to visit her, but Teresa asked her to wait until her Clothing Day.

Finally, on Our Lady's Birthday, 8 September, the Chapter voted unanimously that Sister Teresa should be admitted to the Novitiate and clothed with the Carmelite habit. It came as complete surprise to her, because when she was called into the Chapter, where the Community were solemnly gathered in their white choir cloaks, she had no idea that the vote had already been taken. "Believe me," she wrote to her mother telling her the news, "I thought I had been rejected. When I heard her tell me that I'd been accepted, I don't know what came over me. And our Rev. Mother immediately embraced me, an embrace that lasted a long time, since I didn't let her go, as I couldn't imagine how to thank her. Then I began to hug them all—I almost disarmed them—so much so that they teased me about it later."[8]

The Community had no hesitation in admitting Teresa to her Clothing. As Mother Angelica told Teresa's family, "You have no idea what a girl like Juanita means to us." The Prioress described her as a privileged creature, and even though only one or two sisters knew of the graces she received in prayer, all could see her prayerfulness and unaffected love of God. Mother Angelica painted a portrait of her as she appeared to the Community:

Our little sister, who from her earliest years had exercised herself in acquiring and practicing virtue impelled by her love of Jesus, appeared to have mastered them all. Thus, we could see, it might be said, a consummate prudence and discretion united with an angelic simplicity in this child. In her conversations she expressed herself with naturalness, without reticence, or measuring words. She was affable and joyful. She always strove to hide her intelligence and evident talent, the solid instruction she had received, and the enlightenment on the highest matters which God's grace had given her. She made a concentrated effort in this matter. Using her favorite expression, she "tried to efface herself" and wanted to be overshadowed. She never gave her opinion in anything. She was always ready to concede. She did not display knowledge of anything in matters of prayer, virtue, etc., although she had received instructions in them from God himself.[9]

Her joy in the prospect of receiving the habit overflowed in a long letter she wrote to her friend Graciela, urging her to come for the ceremony and trying to express some of her happiness in her Carmelite vocation:

Get them to bring you for my habit reception, because I'll be happy to see you. Most of all, so you can see for yourself the happiness of being a Carmelite, which is striking me as a more and more significant and growing reality for me. If I used to consider my vocation as above all others, now I appreciate it doubly; because I have seen and experienced for myself that a Carmelite's holiness is greater than any other religious ideal.

.We live for Jesus alone. And just as the angels in heaven incessantly sing His praises, so does a Carmelite

echo these praises here on earth, whether near to the
tabernacle where God who is Love lives imprisoned,
or in the intimate depths of her soul's heaven, where
faith tells her God dwells. Our vocation's objective is
love, the greatest thing a human heart can possess. This
love is a bonfire where the soul is consumed and made
one with her God. That blazing fire permits nothing to
stand in its path, making everything disappear, even
creatures, in order to be united with the infinite fire
of love which is God. This is why a Carmelite seeks
solitude, that nothing may interfere with her union
with the One for whom she left all things. When a soul
truly loves—and this we see even in human love—she
wants only to be with the loved one, gazing always
upon the beloved, sharing the intimacy of her heart,
being drawn ever closer and closer. And this is why
we, who love Jesus with our whole soul, want only to
contemplate and converse with him alone, that his divine ideas and feelings may replace our own miserable
ones ....[10]

Her efforts to encourage her friend were not in vain, because Chela
would herself enter the Los Andes Carmel a few years later, joining
her sister Teresita there.

In the few short weeks before her Clothing, Teresa wrote many
letters to young friends from her school days, who wanted to know
more about the religious life, about prayer, about how she was getting
on in Carmel. It is a measure of her influence and the trust they put in
her, and their realization of her closeness to God. Many of them did
indeed follow her into Carmel, and also into the Sacred Heart Order.

She had a lovely surprise when her own mother joined her in the
Carmelite Order, by becoming a member of the Third Order, an asso-
ciation of those who follow a form of the Carmelite Rule in the world.
Addressing her by her name in religion of Sister Mary Magdalene of

Saint Teresa, Teresa wrote to her mother at the end of September, saying how envious she was that her mother had been clothed in the secular form of the habit, without going through the period of postulancy: "This shows me that Rev. Father Avertano found in you virtues and perfections worthy of a Carmelite. While you enjoy this privilege, your poor sister Teresa finds herself quite poor in virtue, despite her five months of postulancy. How disgraceful! Still, I trust that your prayers will help me to be accepted by Our Lord, so that I may not be quite so unworthy of that very dear habit."[11]

Before her own longed for Clothing day arrived, though, Teresa had the joy of another, Community, retreat given by Father Avertano, which served as her preparation for her Clothing. The notes she wrote on the retreat emphasized her high understanding of her Carmelite vocation, which she also unremittingly described in every letter she wrote from her Carmelite cell. She belonged to God, since he had created her, and therefore she must live only for God and in God. In bringing her to the cloister God had drawn her into this life in himself, since the cloister is the antechamber of heaven and in it God alone exists for the soul.

The purpose of her existence was prayer, and yet she was unworthy even to pronounce the name of Jesus. The high privilege of prayer, and our human duty to engage in it, threw the brightest of light onto her own unworthiness, her "criminal nothingness", and she compared herself to the Samaritan woman, Mary Magdalene, and the woman taken in adultery. Yet he was the Good Shepherd, who forgave them, so she could count on his forgiveness, too. "Oh, my adored Jesus, by your divine Heart, forget my ungratefulness and take me to yourself completely. Free me from all that's going on around me. May I live by always contemplating you. May I live submerged in your love, so that it will consume my miserable being and transform me into you."[12]

Finally, her Clothing Day arrived, on 14 October, the Eve of the Feast of Saint Teresa of Avila, and her friends and family arrived to share the day with her. Mama Ofelia also came to see her beloved charge receive the habit. All except her father, who still could not face the pain of the separation, with her Clothing being yet one more step in that process. Teresa was able to come out for one last time to be with them, before bidding them goodbye once again.

Writing to her father later, she said that this contact with her family and friends had made her realize that there were extremely painful wounds in everyone; that everyone, despite an apparent happiness, carries within them a world of unhappiness. There had been a few deaths in the family that year. Miguel was still driving his mother to distraction. Rebecca was slipping into even greater depression through missing her sister. Luis found his faith even more undermined by his sister's Clothing. Luis himself said that she was radiant with happiness, seeing it as an important step in her effort to give herself over to God, even more convinced of her vocation, filled with a deep peace, even through the pain she shared with her family, because she had with her the One who is the fountain of peace. Her vocation was to pray that this peace and happiness would be communicated to a world that so badly needed it.

Notes

1. *Letter* 116
2. *Letter* 101
3. *Letter* 117
4. *Letter* 114
5. *Letter* 120
6. *Letter* 109
7. *Letter* 128
8. *Letter* 129
9. *Testimonies*, p. 47
10. *Letter* 130
11. *Letter* 135
12. *Diary* 57

Chapter 16
Novitiate

During the months of postulancy the young nun is introduced gradually into the religious life, and is not expected to follow the whole Rule. There follows the year of Novitiate, which is a time where she is expected to follow the Rule more closely, a more intense time of testing for the Community to see whether the aspirant is suited to the life and for the aspirant to see whether it is really the life she wants. To ease the pain of separation, while she was a postulant Teresa was given leave to write often to her family and friends, but now she had to follow the Community rules for letter writing and visits. Normally, family members could visit or receive letters once a month, friends less often, unless there were particular reasons for the rules to be waived.

The purifying of her prayer life intensified. At the beginning of November she wrote to Father Blanch describing her present state:

> The state of my soul is such that I can't define it: one day darkness, distractions, with all my will longing to love, causing me great pain at my inability to love Our Lord, my inability to see Him. Here I can't keep back my tears, because I cry out to my Jesus with such anguish. Another day, I'm able to be recollected in faith, but don't feel anything. All I can do is meditate. This darkness is followed by a bit of light which increases my torment. I also feel my sinfulness and my inconstancy so much that I begin to hate myself, and it seems to me that no one loves me, which causes me to suffer, since I find neither consolation or peace in God or in creatures. I see the immense love of my God, and feel myself incapable of loving Him according to the longings within me. I want to suffer, yet resign myself to the divine will.[1]

Did some news of this darkness of her soul filter through to her family? Her mother must have heard, for Teresa was soon writing to Doña Lucia to reassure her:

> I'm still laughing at all that our Rev. Mother told me is being said in the world about this poor Carmelite. Mommy, why do they want to upset you, telling you that I am sad, I weep, etc.? Why does the world try to awaken the dead for its own sake, finding sadness in those who live in Jesus's arms. Can't they see that it's envy of the repose and of the peace and happiness flooding my soul? How clearly I see that those who invent these kinds of lies don't know what it's like to live in Carmel and what such a vocation really implies! Besides, if in my letters, Mommy, you notice joy and happiness, how can they believe that I'm so duplicitous as to express precisely the opposite of what I feel?[2]

Teresa perfectly embodied the paradox that there could be suffering and darkness of soul, and yet at the same time she could experience the deep happiness of knowing she was within the will of God and where he wanted her to be. Even in the darkness she knew God was working within her, and that her suffering was God's action, carving out greater depths within her to fill her even more fully with himself. So it was that she knew herself as deeply happy, and that she loved him more than life itself. "I'm happy and I shall never cease to be so, for I belong to my God. In Him I find my heaven, my eternal, unchanging love. I want nothing but Him. And this love continues to grow in my soul to the extent that I'm brought into His divine Heart of love and adorable perfections."[3]

The Lord was also purifying her love for her Prioress. There was between the two women a mutual esteem and a genuine loving appreciation of each other—the Prioress aware of the depth of holiness in her young novice, Teresa cherishing the gifts of wisdom and like holiness in her Prioress, who was also her Novice Mistress. But even this understandable and natural affection gave her concern: "I do think I am attached to her, because I think frequently think of what she does and tells me," she explained to Father Blanch. "Besides, I like to be with her, to have her show me love and I feel badly when I notice that she's not so affectionate."[4] However, Our Lord told her that if she wanted to draw closer to him, then even these natural expressions of affection had to go.

Teresa was a naturally outgoing and tactile person and this cost her a great deal, especially as some of the solicitude that Mother Angelica had shown her during her settling in period now had to be withdrawn in the more testing period of the Novitiate. She wrote:

> In my heart I always feel that desire for demonstrations of tenderness. More than ever right now; because Our Lord is not showering them on me. This saddens me because I want to belong to God alone, and to be detached, not only exteriorly but interiorly. It seems to me that desiring those tender gestures is innate to me, because I don't know whether you've noticed that I tend to be rather spoiled and that I'm very childish, which drives me to desperation. But anyway, I've overcome quite a bit of it.[5]

She was very hard on herself. Luis testified that she never had a childish temperament and that he remembered her as always being in control of herself; there were very few occasions when she did give way to herself. And despite her fears over her love for her Prioress, she told Mother Angelica that if she were attached to her, on that day she would leave the convent. Even in expressing her concerns to Father Blanch she was clear-sighted enough to recognize that what drew her to Mother Angelica was her ability to draw her nearer to God. She looked up to her as a saint, and one whose example she could follow. Their talk was of God, which brought her peace. On the one hand she had a duty to open herself up to her Prioress in her role as Novice Mistress, yet on the other hand the Lord was asking her to undergo her purifying interior trials in silence.

On 21 November, Feast of the Presentation of Our Lady in the Temple, the Community renewed their religious vows. Teresa, of course, could not do so as yet, except in her heart, but after the ceremony she went to her cell and wrote out a list of resolutions that she wished to observe to enable her to live out her Carmelite life as totally as possible:

> 1. To live only for God, that is to say, with my thoughts fixed on Him, rejecting everything useless. To live completely hidden from creatures, not speaking anything of self, never giving my opinion on anything unless asked, not calling attention to myself in any way, neither in my manner of speaking or laughing, nor in my expressions, nor even to speak about myself in order to humiliate myself, in a word, that the criminal nothingness may disappear.
>
> 2. To be faithful to all that Jesus is asking of me. To be faithful in the least detail. To be faithful in practicing what I'm advised to do, and to do things with perfection.
>
> 3. To keep silence rigorously during the day and not to speak even with our Mother Superior, unless she first speaks to me.
>
> 4. To live in the present moment with faith.
>
> 5. Never to laugh or make signs to my dear sisters during the day.

6. During recreations to have great dominion over myself so as to be always cheerful, but without transgressing the limits of religious modesty.

7. To consider our Mother Superior like a tabernacle where Jesus is exposed, and my little Sisters as hosts where Jesus dwells in a hidden way. I'll love our Reverend Mother because for me she represents God's authority and His Divine will. I'll love my little Sisters because they are images of God and because Jesus gave me a precept to do so.

8. Not to speak of spiritual things and to act as though I don't understand or grasp anything.

9. Never show that I'm suffering, unless Mother Superior asks me.

10. Never seek consolation in anyone, not even in Jesus, but ask Him to grant me strength to suffer more.

11. To always consider myself despicable, as much by creatures as by God, and to cheerfully accept humiliations, forgetfulness by creatures and by Jesus, without becoming discouraged.

Finally, I'll always strive to do what I believe is most perfect.[6]

As the testimony of her Prioress showed, she kept these resolutions nobly.

In November her family went to Cunaco for their usual summer holiday. Teresa remembered with fondness her holiday there, but did not regret that she was now in Carmel. She had been upset that Rebecca had left school in September, and without gaining her Child of Mary medal, but now she was intent on cheering her sister up, knowing how she would miss her not being there with them in Cunaco.

Advent began on 30 November, when the sisters did not write letters, so in the days leading up to Advent she wrote several letters to friends and family to tide them over until Christmas. She sent feast day greetings to her mother and Lucia, since their feast day of Saint Lucy fell on 13 December. She assured her mother that her health was standing up wonderfully well, and that she had been given a hermitage on the grounds of the monastery which she looked after and could use for prayer. She also asked them to send some crib figures for Christmas, which her sister Lucia actually supplied for her.

To Chubby she wrote a charming and very practical plan of action by which her friend could prepare for the birth of Christ:

> Prepare yourself for the birth of Christ. Think every day, think of Jesus, who, though the eternal God, was born as a fragile Child. Though all-powerful, He was born poor with nowhere to go from the cold. He needed His Mother to live though He was Life itself. I'm sending you a list of things to prepare a set of baby clothes for Jesus; and, when you write, tell me if you did these things.

> Little shirts to keep Him warm: Five acts of love a day and longings to receive Him in Communion. "My Jesus, come to my poor heart, which wants to beat only for You."

> Little blankets to cover His tiny feet: Since He can't walk, you will go and do acts of charity to all, sacrificing yourself and setting aside your own comfort.

> Swaddling bands to wrap around him: Never grumble when they tell you to do something you don't like. Just do what they tell you.

> Little cap: Study and do everything for Jesus, thinking of His love.

Crib: Don't sleep late in bed. Go to Mass and Communion.

Pieces of straw: Do some little act, like giving up candy or eating what you don't like.[7]

The whole family came to see her at Christmas. It was a happy time, when she could see her little niece Lucecita again, but the parting was hard:

> When they come to see me from home and when they leave me here in my little convent, I feel happy that He's the absolute Master of my being," she wrote to Chubby, "happy that He has given me everything, even my own will. But don't think I don't feel the sacrifice, too, because separation is always felt intensely; but that's where the merit is. Isn't love shown through sacrifice? Besides, I think of the love of Jesus and then every sacrifice seems too little. Seeing Him there, I reflect on Him there in the crib among rough straw, warmed by the animals, forgotten by everyone, crying out in the cold; and I ask myself could I be upset by any sacrifice at all?[8]

Perhaps the biggest sacrifice was to see for herself how badly Rebecca was suffering, and was actually going into depression. It was even harder to know that she was the cause of her sister's distress, but she knew, too, that she had to follow the call of Jesus to Carmel. But God can work through such situations, as Teresa herself knew only too well, and she prayed and discerned that God was indeed working out his purposes in Rebecca, too. She wrote to her mother:

> I couldn't help but being moved to pity seeing all she suffers. Believe me, Mummy, perhaps had I been in her place I might not have been as generous as she. Jesus had to clothe me with His grace to follow Him,

as I would never have left you all, loving you as I do. Right now it seems to me that it's necessary to surround her with love and not get her upset, since I think she's feeling worse and worse. I also see God working in her soul through loneliness, in order to draw her to Himself; and I'm more convinced each day that God will make her completely His.[9]

To Rebecca herself, she used a carrot and stick approach. She pointed out that she should come out of herself a bit more, and recognize that she had to think of others: "Do you think that just because people contradict you or don't give in to your wishes that they don't love you? Then I could say the same thing. When I was at home I had to go against the same things by my own will even in slight things. Don't think it wasn't hard for me sometimes to have to accommodate myself to the wishes of others."[10]

Now that Rebecca had left school and was at home, she had to take over some of the responsibilities that Teresa had once had, and she was obviously finding it irksome. On the other hand, Teresa encouraged her with what she could discern of God's workings in Rebecca: "I want you to know how happy I am to belong to God alone, and I'll tell you a secret: I see God working marvelously in your soul to draw you to Himself, taking you away from the ones you love so much, separating you away from everything so that you may find your only support in Him."[11] Small comfort, perhaps, at this particular point, but Teresa was discerning the future for her beloved sister.

The community had several days of recreation over Christmas before going back to the usual routine, while her family went to Algarrobo for more holidays, although once more her father was unable to go with them. Once again, Teresa was disappointed when her father failed to turn up on a visiting day, when she had been assured he would most definitely come. His business affairs were still going from bad to worse, his crops not doing well, and life was an uphill struggle all the time. In contrast, Teresa's crops of vegetables and flowers in her monastic garden were flourishing. Teresa tried to urge him to join the rest of the family for a break: "Why don't you go at least for fifteen days to swim in the ocean?" she wrote to him. "Don't kill yourself with all that heat and with all that work. Go, Daddy dear, and rest with your children and with Mum, because you greatly need the rest. I also beg you not to delay your meal times. And the same goes for sleep; try to get enough. Listen to your Carmelite daughter, since she'll be praying things go well with you."[12] Her mother had obviously been pouring out her concerns over the way her husband was neglecting himself.

By the time Lent was due to begin, when once again the community didn't write or receive letters, Teresa still hadn't heard from her father, so she tried again, hoping another letter would prompt him to reply before Lent. She so longed to hear from him. Instead, Miguel, who was better at writing and was working with his father, wrote to her giving her bits of news, though she still didn't know how well their harvest or their business was going.

There was another reason why she so desperately wanted to hear from her father before Lent began. Just before Lent she had received inner awareness that she had only a few weeks to live, and that if her father didn't write to her then, he would never be able to do so.

Notes

1. *Letter* 145
2. *Letter* 148
3. Ibid.
4. *Letter* 145
5. Ibid.
6. *Diary* 58

7. *Letter* 156
8. Ibid.
9. Ibid.
10. *Letter* 159
11. Ibid.
12. *Letter* 157

Chapter 17
Last Days

The season of Lent began, and Teresa threw herself into the penitential practices with enthusiasm. She so longed to share the cross with her beloved Lord, to be a little Cyrenian, as she put it. Mother Angelica said it was difficult not to grant her every request to perform penances. It was as Holy Week began that her sickness began to be noticed, although she did not spare herself in any way. She had always prayed on her knees, whether she was in her cell or in Choir. She spent almost the whole of Holy Thursday in prayer, and then, after the solemn Mass was finished and the Blessed Sacrament reserved for adoration, as the Church remembered Christ's Agony in the Garden, she spent the night until one o'clock in the morning watching with her Lord. If she had been allowed to do so, she would have spent the whole night there. "What went on that day between her soul and God is unknown," Mother Angelica wrote in testimony, "But she was in recollection or deep contemplation and was so absorbed that on calling her in the night that she was to go to bed, one could see the violence that was needed for her to return to herself."[1] In fact, by the time Teresa got to her cell, she felt so tired that she was too weary to fall asleep, and only got four hours sleep.

On Good Friday she got up at the usual time and followed the solemn Holy Week liturgy and the regular observance in every detail. At noon there was a period of prayer and meditation of the Three Hours,[2] where she sang strongly with her beautiful and resonant voice. She remained in Choir after the liturgy had finished, kneeling in prayer before the Crucifix exposed on the altar.

It was only some time later, when she had returned to her cell, that Mother Angelica felt urged to go to Sister Teresa's cell. She noticed that Teresa's face was very red, which was unusual, and thought she might have a fever, and immediately ordered her to go to bed. To begin with, she was given medicine that they already had in the house, while the doctor was called. It was only when the doctor asked how long she had felt unwell that Teresa revealed that she had felt ill for about a month. She had accepted it as an extra penance, but now felt guilty that she had hidden it and profoundly asked forgiveness. However, the community didn't know that she had already told Father Avertano, her spiritual director, at the beginning of March that her death would be painful and would occur in April. If this was the will of God for her, then she would not impede that will.

Mother Angelica had Sara Urbistondo, the extern, telephone Teresa's mother to tell her of her daughter's illness, and Doña Lucia immediately sent her own doctor, Diaz Lira, to the monastery.

Six doctors in all were called in to try and reduce the fever, without success. Teresa had contracted typhus, for which there was then no cure. Even now, the illness has to be detected early and treatment given immediately if there is to be hope of a cure. After infection with the disease there is an incubation period of about two weeks, and it is only then that a person is aware of feeling ill. Teresa had already gone into the final, fatal stage.

On Monday she asked to go to confession, although it wasn't thought at this point that she was dying. However, the confessor was immediately called for, and she received the Sacrament of Confession, and then Holy Communion, remaining absorbed in prayer for over an hour afterwards.

By this time she was slipping in and out of consciousness and was sometimes delirious with fever and convulsions, so on the following day she again received Holy Communion and was also given Extreme Unction. Her mother, being told of the gravity of her illness, took the earliest train to come and visit her. In order to spare the monastery the expense of doctor's fees, Doña Lucia wanted to take her daughter away from the monastery and came with the necessary permission from the Nuncio. She also offered to bring in the best doctors there were in Santiago. Mother Angelica explained to her that if she did take Teresa out of the monastery she would not die as a religious, something that would cause Teresa immense distress. They assured Doña Lucia that everything possible was being done for her within the monastery. The sisters were keeping continual watch beside her bed, and giving her every possible care. Teresa had in fact told her mother some time before that she knew she would die young, but this did not in any way mitigate the devastating news.

On 7 April it was diagnosed that Teresa had perforated typhus in its advanced stages, and Mother Angelica suggested to her, during one of her periods of lucidity, that she could make her religious vows. Around 12:30 in the afternoon that day she became fully conscious and lucid, and with great joy took her vows of poverty, chastity and obedience, vows that she had for so long observed so faithfully. She repeated the profession of vows three times in a strong, clear voice, and expressed her joy and gratitude to her beloved community who had gathered around her bedside. She also received Communion, for the last time, as it turned out, for the following morning her delirium entered its most severe and intense stage. The typhus had taken an unusual form, and its rapid advance surprised her doctors.

Throughout her illness Teresa retained her extraordinary self-control in the face of intense pain, a self-control so lovingly practiced over so many years of surrender to God and in her willing embrace of the cross in whatever form it came. Even drinking the smallest amount of water became a torment to her. "One never heard her complain through all this or ask for anything which would relieve the pain,"

Mother Angelica testified. "She accepted everything and refused nothing, painful though it might be. She did not show the least desire, not even for changing her position or even for drinking a little water. She never indicated what might be bothering her. And the infirmarians do not remember her giving them the least hint in this sense. She obeyed, even concerning the most painful and mortifying thing. She always had a smile on her lips and a thankful word for her sisters. Sister Teresa believed herself unworthy of such attention and care."[3] The sisters, of course, could not do enough for her, in anguish that they were going to lose so soon a sister who had become so dear to them.

Sometimes Teresa tried to kneel and ask forgiveness for what she had always termed her "criminal nothingness," the Lord purifying her of even the slightest stain that still remained through the sufferings for which she had always longed, and which she now greeted with her customary joy. It was also evident that she was deeply united with Our Lord in prayer, often repeating a word he had given to her earlier on: "The victim of love must climb to Calvary." Like Saint Thérèse of Lisieux, she, too, was fulfilling her vocation of being a victim of love.

Beginning on Saturday night her agony intensified, and the whole community gathered round her bedside. Father Avertano came frequently to give her absolution, and on Sunday there was a small rally. Her beloved brother Luis also came to Los Andes to see his sister. During the celebration of Mass she sang the "Asperges" in her beautiful voice, and she was also able to recognize one of her sisters and greeted her happily. In the afternoon she appeared to sleep, but this was in fact a coma from which she would not awake until the moments before her death.

The following day, Monday, 12 April, it was obvious that her last moments were near. The Community, with the chaplain, again gathered around her bedside to recite the prayers for the dying. She recovered consciousness as her final moments approached. Sister Isabel of the Trinity, Teresa's fellow novice, was at the foot of the bed, and described her final moments: "She had her gaze turned upward: her face shining, and she radiated an immense peace and joy like someone who is being caught up into God."[4] At 7:15 in the evening, she gently gave her last breath as Father Avertano was giving her his final absolution.

Notes

1. *Testimonies*, p. 50
2. This was before the reform of the Liturgy; at that time the Solemn Good Friday Liturgy celebrated at 3 p.m.
3. *Testimonies*, p. 53
4. *Testimonies*, p. 86

Chapter 18
First Fruits

"To die is to be eternally immersed in Love," Teresa had written. She was now with the Lord she loved so much, and her new apostolate was about to begin.

After washing her and clothing her in the habit, the sisters brought Teresa down to the Choir so that her family could view her through the grille. She wore the white mantle, and her white novice's veil, which was now surrounded by a crown of white roses. The sisters had also scattered white roses over her body.

The whole family came to Los Andes for the funeral. Her mother was the first to approach the grille and pay her respects to her beloved daughter; her father at last came to the Carmel, able to see his daughter now only in death.

The funeral took place two days later, on Wednesday, 14 April. At first, the family wanted to take the body back to Santiago for burial, but they were easily persuaded that Teresa would have wanted to be buried with her Carmelite family. All the family was there, as well as a great many of her friends. What nobody had foreseen was that crowds of people who had never even met Teresa also came. The church was filled to overflowing, and the crowd spilled out on to the pavement outside, and down the street. There was an electric sense that something special had happened, that a saint had died. So crowded was the church that the twelve priests who also attended to celebrate the Mass had trouble in passing through to the altar. People passed their rosaries and other religious objects through the grille to touch her body, and afterwards refused to leave the Chapel, overwhelmed by the sense that they had participated in some very special occasion.

There were fears that Mother Angelica would be unable to attend the funeral, as she was running a high fever, but at the last moment she was pronounced well enough by her doctor to assist at the Mass. Luis saw his sister's body, and felt crushed as he gazed on her face that looked as if she was simply sleeping. "She seemed to sleep so gently," Sister Gabriel of the Child Jesus testified. "Her face, with the majesty of death, seemed to keep an expression of supernatural peace that inspired veneration in those who beheld it."[1]

Years before, the Lord had promised Teresa that she should resign herself to not seeing the fruit of her prayers for her family. Now, after her death, her prayers would begin to bear fruit.

Rebecca was the first answer to her prayer, and the funeral was a turning point. The black depression from which she had been suffering ever since her sister's entry into Carmel suddenly lifted. Her health, both physical and mental, recovered, and she began to follow the course which she had been dimly discerning and which Teresa had also discerned, that the Lord was calling her to Carmel, too. She entered the Los Andes Carmel later that year, on 23 November. Over the years, she carefully gathered all the materials on her sister that she could, letters, photographs, and above all her diary. She died in the odor of sanctity on 31 December 1942.

Her father, who had lapsed in the practice of his faith due to the pressures of his work and the collapse in the family finances, also found his way back. He died a holy death three years later in Hualane.

After Mass, Luis, to his confusion and some embarrassment, found people pointing to him, saying, "That is the brother of a saint." His sense of loss of the beloved sister on whom he had depended emotionally so much was overwhelming. Death, he felt, had robbed him irrevocably of her, and his bitterness increased. Nevertheless, at the funeral a shaft of light pierced his darkness and it was the beginning of his gradual return to the faith, even though it took many years. He visited her grave many times as the years passed and saw increasing numbers of people praying there. He heard many stories and accounts of miracles worked through her intercession, and answers to prayer. For him, though, the great miracle remained her angelic life and her intense love of Christ; and the greatest miracle she worked was in him, breaking through his "cruel doubts," as he described them, due to his reading in philosophy, to bring him back to faith.

Luis did indeed see his sister one last time, when, in 1940, the Community was preparing to move to their new monastery on Sarmiento Street. Teresa's body was disinterred, and Bishop Bernadino Berrios invited Luis and Rebecca to identify the remains. Luis was very moved to see that in her hands was a little rosary of his that he had given her years before. As a lovely gesture, the Bishop, who was also present, told brother and sister to embrace each other, for one short time not separated by Carmel's grilles.

Luis returned to the practice of his faith shortly before his death in 1984. He ended his testimony with this poignant admission: "It is difficult for a brother to judge Juanita's place in history. I can only remember her with reverence. Yet I am still overcome by a humble pride of knowing that Juanita's blood is also my blood."[2]

Miguel, too, saw the fruit of his sister's prayers. Despite Doña Lucia's despair of him, he did actually have a deep faith. Putting his wild life behind him, he married. He had two children, lived a very Christian life, and died in 1947.

The Community was devastated at losing such a promising and deeply loved sister. "We watched her pass as a ray of light, like a vision," wrote Mother Angelica, who knew more than most the depth of her young novice's holiness. "Her absence has left a most profound sorrow in our hearts, but we have thanked the Lord for having drawn her to our monastery and for having permitted us to contemplate sanctity in such a young girl."[3]

But that sanctity was not to remain hidden. The crowds that attended her funeral did not diminish. There was a consistent and steady stream of visitors who came to visit her grave. Claims of miracles, cures and answers to prayers continued. However much Luis said he was not a believer, he was certainly able to put his finger on spiritual realities. Seeing the people consistently seeking out his sister, convinced of her holiness, he remarked: "I can find only one explanation. In their wisdom, Christian people, guided by God, sense when there is true virtue and holiness."[4] They are aided in this by "the secret inner fire of the Holy Spirit who keeps the world alive."[5]

Two years after her death, a Jesuit who lived in the same community as Father Colom approached the Carmel and said he considered that the matter of her canonization should be presented to the local bishop. Father Colom had often spoken to him of his young penitent, and contrary to his usual practice, had also kept all the letters Teresa had written to him. The Community needed no convincing over Teresa's holiness, but had felt that they should not take the first step. Now, encouraged by the Jesuit priest, matters were put in hand and progressed rapidly. Twenty-seven years after her death the cause of beatification was begun. For her to be declared Blessed, after her life had been thoroughly investigated, a miracle was required. The one that was approved was the cure of a young fireman, Hector Uribe Carrasco, who was accidentally electrocuted during a fire rescue. Doctors declared him clinically dead, and his family and friends turned to Teresa's intercession. Within a few minutes vital signs began to reappear and he was completely restored to health on 8 December, a day that meant so much to Teresa.

Pope John Paul II beatified her on 3 April 1987, during his visit to Chile, describing her as a young Chilean girl, symbol of the faith and goodness of this people, captivated by the heavenly Kingdom in the springtime of her youth, the first fruits of the holiness of the Teresian Carmelites in Latin America. Time and again, the Pope returned to Teresa's saying that God is infinite joy. This affected her in her natural youth and high spirits. "She was full of vitality and cheerfulness, never lacking a sense of healthy amusement, play, and contact with nature, just a true daughter of her time. She was a happy and dynamic girl, open to God." But this natural vitality was given depth by her happiness and total dedication to God:

> Teresa of Los Andes irradiates the joy of those who are poor in spirit, meek and humble of heart, of those who suffer in silence, for this is how God purifies and sanctifies his chosen ones. She hungers and thirsts for justice, for she loves God intensely and wants him to be loved and known by all. In her complete immolation, God made her have compassion for priests and for the conversion of sinners. Peaceful and reconciling, she shows understanding and dialogues with all around her. Her life above all reflects the beatitude of purity of heart. In effect, she surrenders her life totally to Christ and Jesus opened her eyes to the contemplation of his mysteries."6

A further miracle was needed for her canonization, and the miracle chosen was that of the resuscitation of a twelve year old girl, Marcella Antúnes, who had drowned in a swimming pool, and was returned to life through Teresa's intercession. She was present at Teresa's canonization in Saint Peter's Basilica on 21 March 1993. Appropriately, this was the fourth Sunday of Lent, Laetare Sunday, which the Pope said could well be called the day of light. In his homily the Pope stressed this theme of light in his description of Teresa's life:

> God made shine forth in her in an admirable way the light of his Son Jesus Christ, so that she could be a beacon and guide a world that seems to be blind to the splendor of the divine. In a secularized society, which turns its back on God, this Chilean Carmelite, whom to my great joy I present as a model of the perennial youth of the Gospel, gives shining witness of a life which proclaims to the men and women of our day that it is in loving, adoring and serving God that the human person finds greatness and joy, freedom and fulfillment. The life of the Blessed Teresa cries out continually from within her cloister "God alone suffices."

She shouts it out particularly to the young people who hunger for the truth and seek a light which will give direction to their lives. To young people who are being allured by the continuous messages and stimuli of an erotic culture, a society which mistakes the hedonistic exploitation of another for genuine love, which is self-giving, this young virgin of the Andes today proclaims the beauty and happiness that comes from a pure heart.

In her tender love for Christ, Teresa found the essence of the Christian message: to love, suffer, pray, and to serve. In the bosom of her family she learned to love God above all things. In feeling that she belonged to the Creator alone, her love of neighbor became more intense and definitive. She stated as much in one of her letters: "When I love it is for always. A Carmelite never forgets. From her small cell she accompanies souls wherever they are in the world."[7]

Now, in eternity, St. Teresa of Los Andes continues to intercede as an advocate for an endless number of brothers and sisters. What she found in her heaven on earth as a spouse of Jesus, she now contemplates without veil or shadow, and from her immediate closeness, she intercedes for those who seek the light of Christ.

Notes

1. *Testimonies*, p. 92
2. *Testimonies*, p. 55
3. *Testimonies*, p. 87
4. *Testimonies*, p. 15
5. Quoted in *God the Joy of My Life*, p. 322
6. Quoted in *God the Joy of My Life*, p. 333 ff.
7. Quoted in *God the Joy of My Life*, p. 334

Bibliography

God the Joy of My Life: A Biography of Saint Teresa of Jesus of the Andes. Michael D. Griffin O.C.D. Hubertus, WI: Teresian Charism Press. 1995. 3rd rev. ed.

A New Hymn to God. Comp. Michael D. Griffin O.C.D. Hubertus, WI: Teresian Charism Press. 1993.

Testimonies to Saint Teresa of the Andes. Comp. Michael D. Griffin O.C.D. Hubertus, WI: Teresian Charism Press. 1991. 2nd rev. ed.

Letters of Saint Teresa of Jesus of the Andes. Trans. Michael D. Griffin O.C.D. Hubertus WI: Teresian Charism Press. 1994

The Collected Works of Saint John of the Cross. Trans. Kieran Kavanagh O.C.D. and Otilio Rodriguez O.C.D. Washington, DC: ICS Publications. 1973.

Blessed Elizabeth of the Trinity, Carmelite. *I Have Found God*. Complete Works of Elizabeth of The Trinity, Volume 2: *Letters From Carmel.* Trans. Anne Englund Nash. Washington, DC: ICS Publications. 1995.

St Thérèse of Lisieux by those who knew her. Ed. and trans. Christopher O'Mahoney, O.C.D. Dublin: Veritas Publications. 1975.

The Institute of Carmelite Studies promotes research and publication in the field of Carmelite spirituality. Its members are Discalced Carmelites, part of a Roman Catholic community—friars, nuns, and laity—who are heirs to the teaching and way of life of Teresa of Jesus and John of the Cross, men and women dedicated to contemplation and to ministry in the Church and the world. Information concerning their way of life is available through local diocesan Vocation Offices or from the Vocation Directors' Offices:

1233 So. 45th Street, W. Milwaukee, WI 53214

P.O. Box 3420, San Jose, CA 95156-3420

5151 Marylake Drive, Little Rock, AR 72206